Shopping in Marrakech

• • ● • •

SHOPPING in MARRAKECH

by SUSAN SIMON

Photos by Nally Bellati

THE LITTLE BOOKROOM
NEW YORK

© 2009 The Little Bookroom

Text © Susan Simon

Photographs © Nally Bellati

Book design: Jessica Hische / Louise Fili Ltd.

Cover and interior embroidery by Jessica Hische

Library of Congress Cataloging-in-Publication Data

Simon, Susan

Shopping in Marrakech / by Susan Simon; photographs by Nally Bellati.

p. cm.

Includes index.

ISBN 978-1-892145-78-9 (alk. paper)

1. Shopping — Morocco — Marrakech. I. Bellati, Nally. II. Title.

TX337.M82M377 2009

381'.1096464 — dc22

2008041461

Published by The Little Bookroom

435 Hudson Street, 3rd Floor

New York, NY 10014

editorial @ littlebookroom.com

www.littlebookroom.com

10 9 8 7 6 5 4 3 2 1

Printed in China

Distributed in the U.S. by Random House, in the U.K. and Ireland
by Signature Book Services, and in Europe by Random House International.

• • ● • •

For my friend John, who made it easy
for me to come back to Marrakech

again, and again.

• • ● • •

TABLE of CONTENTS

• • ◉ • •

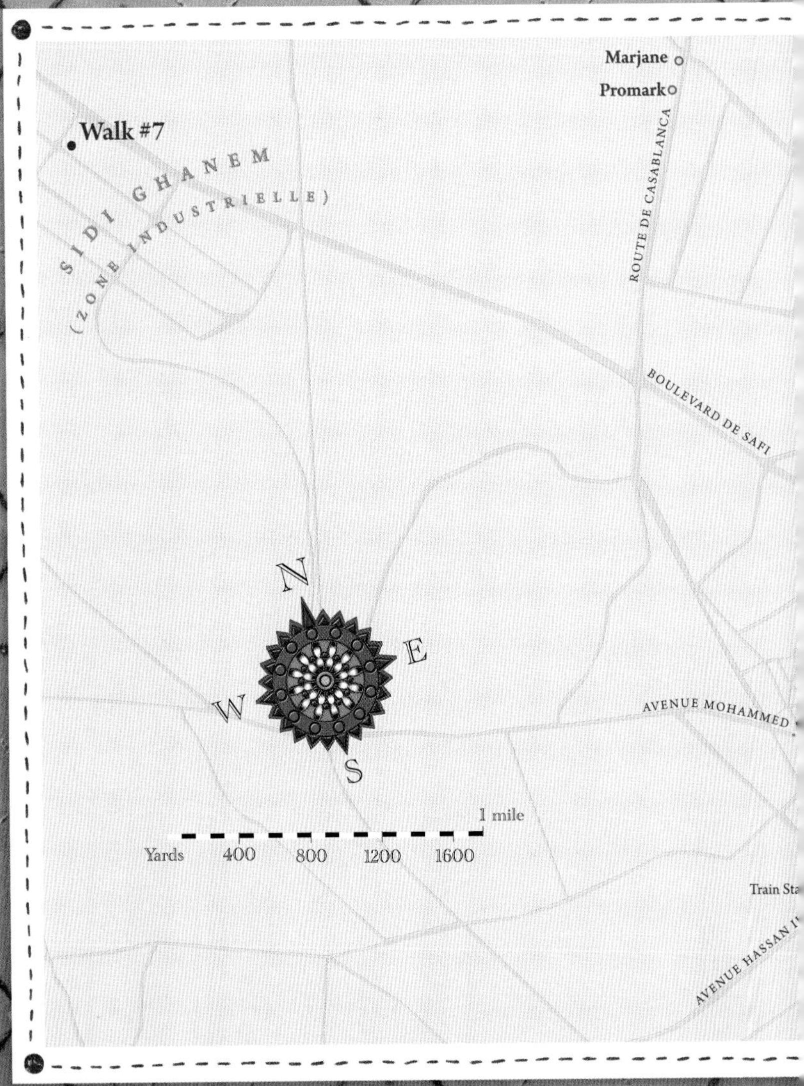

Marjane ○

Promark ○

Walk #7

SIDI GHANEM
(ZONE INDUSTRIELLE)

ROUTE DE CASABLANCA

BOULEVARD DE SAFI

N

W   E

S

AVENUE MOHAMMED

1 mile

Yards   400   800   1200   1600

Train Sta

AVENUE HASSAN I

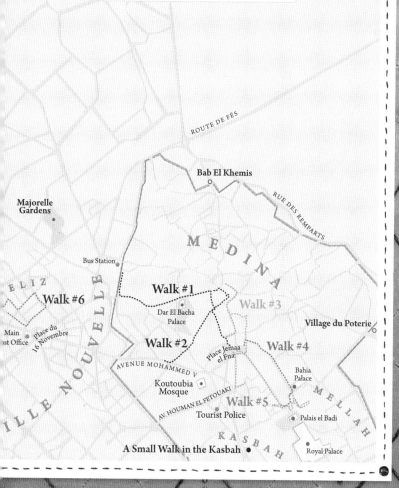

MARRAKECH

ROUTE DE FÈS

Bab El Khemis

RUE DES REMPARTS

Majorelle Gardens

Bus Station

M E D I N A

Walk #1

Walk #3

ELIZ

Walk #6

Dar El Bacha Palace

Village du Poterie

Main Post Office   Place du 16 Novembre

Walk #2

Place Jemaa el Fna

Walk #4

Bahia Palace

VILLE NOUVELLE

AVENUE MOHAMMED V

Koutoubia Mosque

M E L L A H

AV. HOUMAN EL FETOUAKI

Walk #5

Tourist Police

Palais el Badi

K A S B A H

A Small Walk in the Kasbah

Royal Palace

INTRODUCTION

I came to Marrakech for the first time in 1970. My sister Laura and I drove from our home in Milan, Italy, across the southern coast of France, down to the bottom of Spain's southeastern coast, parked the car in the town of Algeciras, and took a ferry the short seven-mile distance to Tangier, Morocco. From Tangier we hopped on the Marrakech Express, the train made famous by a song, and arrived in the city where "Colored cottons hang in the air, charming cobras in the square, striped djellabas we can wear at home…" Crosby, Stills & Nash had seduced an entire generation of travelers with their song, "Marrakech Express."

At the time, Marrakech was one of the last stops on a popular hippie traveling route that wended its way from northern Europe to this oasis-city at the edge of the Sahara desert. I stayed with a college friend at his apartment on the Rue du Commerce in the Mellah—the city's Jewish neighborhood, and Laura stayed at one of the cheap tourist hotels in the main square, the Jemaa el Fna. I think that I remember—through a haze of hashish—that we spent a good deal of time either sitting at cafés in the square drinking mint tea or sticky, sweet café au lait, while being mesmerized by the snake charmers, the Senegalese storytellers, and the cacophonous water sellers—or hanging out on rooftops waiting for the sun to do its thing and set in a spectacular blaze of color behind the snow-capped Atlas Mountains.

And, I shopped. Ever since the Almoravid (an eleventh-century Berber tribe) Youssef ben Tachfine conquered Spain, then with the prescience of the general that he was, placed a trading post/oasis in this strategic location between the sea, mountains, and desert—enclosing it with persimmon-colored ramparts—Marrakech has been a significant spot for the exchange of merchandise. For centuries camel caravans plied the north-south trade route from Spain through the Sahara to

Senegal, Mali, Mauritania, and Ghana and back again. The vestiges of those days are apparent not only in the custom of trade that flourishes to this day but also in the foundouks—the inns that were rest stops for the camels and their drivers. Many of the foundouks have been restored and are now centers dedicated to the preservation of Moroccan arts and crafts.

During my first trip to Marrakech, I bought a tagine dish that has traveled with me for four decades. It now sits on a shelf in my New York City kitchen, seasoned from tagines made with vegetables in Italy, fish on Nantucket, and everything else in New York. I bought a small black-on-black embroidered leather bag fastened to a long tasseled cord that I pull out when I need something small and elegant to wear out in the evening. There was a wool djellabah that long ago succumbed to moths, and a silver Berber cape pin that I bought as a gift for a dear friend, which still sits in his drawer.

Thirty-five years after that first trip to Marrakech, I went back again at the invitation of another friend who had taken a long-term lease on a riad—a house with a courtyard—in the Kasbah, practically around the corner from my first Moroccan residence. I was surprised—oh, that's putting it mildly—I was stunned to see the transformation of Marrakech—that haze that I had attributed to hashish had come, it seems, partially from all the dust that was created from the unpaved derbs, alleys that create the labyrinth of streets of the Medina ("inside the walls"), and the huge dust bowl, Jemaa el Fna, the central square of the city—all of which are now paved with large cement tiles. The population has grown and grown and with it so has the city outside the walls. But the blinding colors, spicy fragrances, and grinning, friendly population—always ready with a greeting of the day in numerous languages—had remained as I remembered. I fell for Marrakech all over again. Three years after the second trip, I went back again—this time to do the research for this book.

There is a unique satisfaction when you tour a spot with a single-subject focus. Oh joy, my subject was shopping! Shopping in Marrakech is dizzying to say the least and downright hallucinatory to say the most. How would I choose amongst the thousands of shops, stores, and souk stalls? It's impossible. Since Marrakech, both inside and outside the walls, is smaller than it appears to be on a map, it is easy to navigate on foot. To further ease the confusion, I've divided this guide into seven separate walks—and little bonus walks—that will bring you through the main shopping areas. As you walk, there will be a variety of shops along each route. As you study the notated maps, you'll be able, should you choose, to create your own path because of the way that the walks crisscross each other. Mix and match. If your time in Marrakech is limited, read through the guide before you set off and pinpoint your areas of real interest. If doing this on your own is too daunting, I recommend two excellent shopping guides (page 14) who will allow your experience to be worry-free.

There are other worries that are often expressed by Moroccan-bound shoppers. One is, "How do I bargain?" The straightforward answer is to not view the exercise as life or death. Be sure that you really want the object before you begin your negotiations. Then offer what you think is a realistic price. When and if you get close to your desired price and there is, say, a 20- or 25-dirham separation, give it to the seller. Life's too short to stand on ceremony for a few dollars. Be prepared to sometimes, but rarely, be screamed at by a highly dramatic seller feigning insult at the price you've offered. Try walking away—he may reconsider. There are more and more shops that advertise *prix fixe* sales. This gives the bargaining question an easy answer. No. Following directly on the heels of bargaining, among traveler concerns, is hassling. Aside from the occasional tap on the shoulder, hassling has just about disappeared from the souks. In 1999, the new king, Mohammed VI, instituted *la brigade touristique*—the tourist police roam the souks in plainclothes keeping an eye out for over-zealous merchants. Aggressive behavior is not tolerated in Marrakech and is punishable by law. If you feel that you're being unfairly treated, it's enough to whip out your mobile phone, pretend to dial the number listed on page 15 and say "police" loudly. It works like a charm.

While many shops say that they take credit cards, it isn't always true. They certainly don't take American Express (there are minor exceptions) despite the occasional Amex sticker on a shop window. Aside from the shops in the Ville Nouvelle, called Gueliz, those in the Zone Industrielle, also called Sidi Ghanem, and some of the major destination shops, cash is king. There are ATM machines located around the Place Jemaa el Fna, and on the Avenue Mohamed V in Gueliz.

Shop hours vary. In the souks it's pretty much a seven days a week, early in the morning to 8 or 9pm operation. In the Mellah, shops are open from morning through the evening except on Friday afternoon when the Muslim Sabbath is observed. In Gueliz most everyone seems to keep European hours, so they close for lunch at 12:30 or 1pm, then re-open at 2:30 or 3 until 7:30pm. Everyone in Gueliz is closed on Sunday.

A smattering of French will serve you well in Morocco although more and more people speak English. If you learn only one word in Arabic it should be *shukran* pronounced as it's spelled; it means "thank you."

Interestingly, Morocco is a rather short flight from the east coast of the States. There's a daily Royal Air Maroc flight from New York that will get you to Casablanca in just under seven hours. In Casablanca you transfer to another plane that will have you in Marrakech in 30 minutes. The time difference between New York and Marrakech is four hours. With very little shock to your body, you can be in a completely exotic spot that's closer to the States than Europe—but, oh so far away culturally.

As Winston Churchill once said about his favorite place on earth, "If you have one day to spend in Morocco, spend it in Marrakech…it's the most lovely spot in the world."

SHOPPING GUIDES

Elena Masera

Tel: 212 070 11 09 93
Email: ELENAMASERA@MSN.COM

Italian, Elena has lived in Marrakech since 2002. She speaks Italian, English, French, and Spanish. She lives in the Medina and knows the souks as if they were her own backyard—which they are. She's also familiar with all the established and latest shops in Gueliz and the Zone Industrielle. She's a warm and accommodating guide who charges by the day or half-day, And she'll arrange for a car and driver for trips outside the Medina.

Maryam Montague

BEST CONTACTED BY **Email:** MARYAM@MTDS.COM

American, Maryam has lived in Marrakech with her architect husband and two children since 2001. The energetic multi-tasker is a travel and lifestyle writer—her book based on her popular blog, "My Marrakesh" will be published by Artisan in 2010. Maryam, an expert shopper for the souks, Gueliz, and Sidi Ghanem (the industrial zone), is English- and French-speaking. Maryam accommodates the most unusual shopping requests. She charges by the day or half-day; services include a car and driver.

Maryam owns a delightful shop of her own, Peacock Pavilions, that includes a personal selection of colorful, and wildly patterned housewares from all over Africa. Again, contact her through email for directions.

Tourist Police

If you ever feel threatened, think you've paid too much for a souvenir, a meal, or a hotel, or are hassled by overzealous merchants, call the number above, or just say "police" out loud. It's likely that one member of this vigilant group of 80 plainclothes policemen will be somewhere nearby. They are all around the Medina. Go to them with any grievance you may have.

WALK № 1

• • ● • •

Rue Mouassine, Rue Dar El Bacha, Rue Bab Doukkala

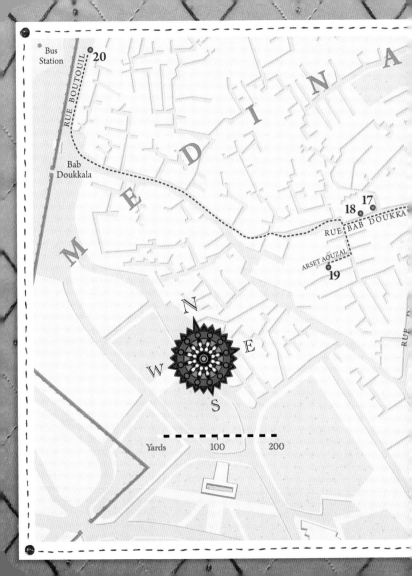

Bus
Station

RUE BOUTOUIL

20

M E D I N A

Bab
Doukkala

18 **17**
RUE BAB DOUKKA

ARSET AOUZAL

19

RUE

N
W — E
S

Yards   100   200

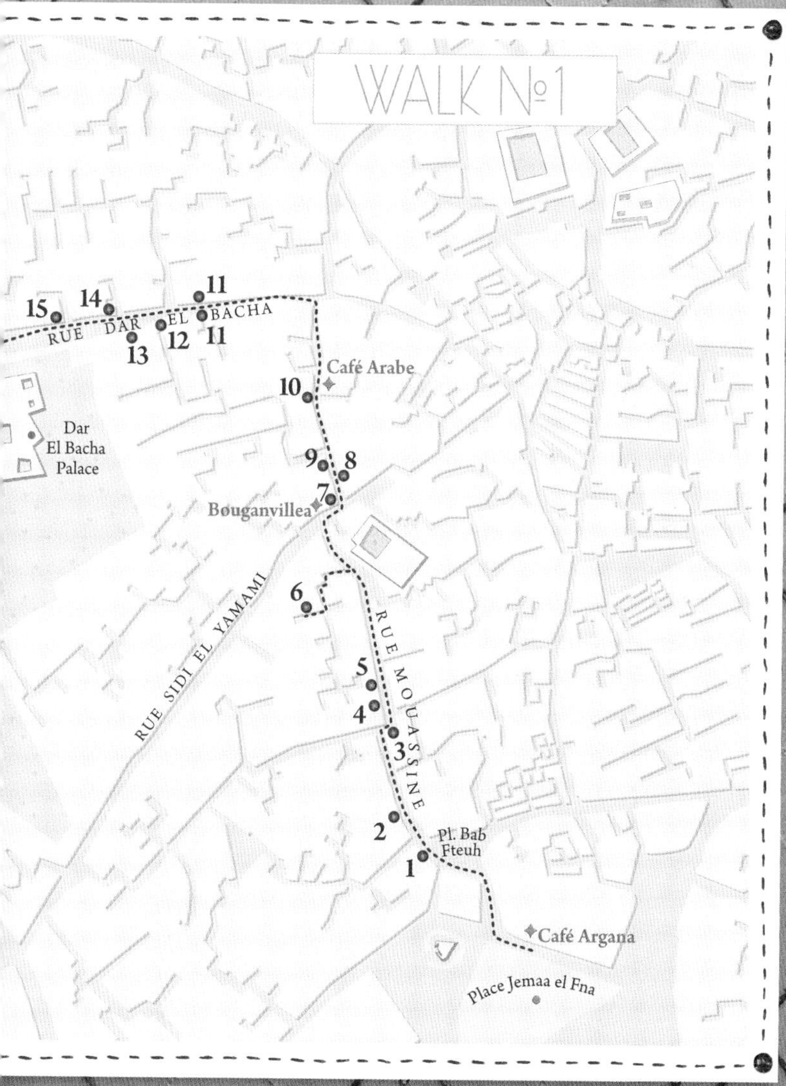

WALK Nº1

RUE DAR EL BACHA

15 14 13 12 11 11

Dar El Bacha Palace

10 Café Arabe

9 8

7

Bouganvillea

6

RUE SIDI EL YAMAMI

5

4

3

RUE MOUASSINE

2

1 Pl. Bab Fteuh

Café Argana

Place Jemaa el Fna

Use the **Café Argana** ◆ on the northwest side of the Place Jemaa el Fna as your point of departure. You may even want to jump-start your walk with a glass of freshly squeezed orange juice, a tiny glass of sweet mint tea, or a café au lait while sitting on Argana's vantage-point terrace.

Sneak around the left side of the café into a broad passageway that will lead you into the small Place Bab Fteuh. Directly to the left, begin your journey down one of the most stylish streets in the Medina, Rue Mouassine.

1. Beldi

9 AND 11 RUE LAKSOUR ♦ **Tel: 212 024 44 10 76**
ALL CREDIT CARDS EXCEPT AMEX
DAILY 9:30AM – 1PM AND 4–7PM

The address is advertised as Rue Laksour, but the entrance is on the Rue Mouassine. Find it on your left just after you leave Place Bab Fteuh. You'll see the word *beldi* in many applications as you roam the city—it means traditional, old, or antique in Arabic. In this tiny shop, you'll find that *beldi* refers to the traditional Moroccan methods that brothers Toufik and Abdelhafid use to make their haute couture versions of caftans, babouches (slippers), bags, and jewelry. Since their father opened

the shop doors in the late 1940s, Beldi has been a destination for style-conscious women and men. It's important to note that this shop is a favorite not only of visitors but of Moroccans as well. Of particular interest are the caftans made of velvet, and of Moroccan "cashmere"—a fine brushed cotton—lined in tissue silk, then decorated with intricate embroidery, as well as crushed silk babouches and bags, and highly embroidered "cashmere" blankets. Have a look at the exquisite white bed linens trimmed with colorful, traditional embroidery—you may just find them irresistible as well.

2. Men's Clothing Courtyard

CASH ONLY ● DAILY

When you leave Beldi, keep an eye out for an archway, on the left that leads into a large courtyard. You'll know that you're in the right place if you see stalls selling fabric by the meter, and ones that specialize in men's clothing. Directly opposite the entrance across the courtyard is a shoebox-sized shop that has the most interesting selection for men. Find soft-as-a-cloud white Moroccan "cashmere" caftans, white heavy cotton kandrissi — the billowing men's pants that are fitted below the knee, and loose fitting pants that men wear under their long caftans. These elastic-waist pants have zippered side pockets that provide a storage area for money, keys, etc., that the pocketless—with only slit openings—caftans can't. These pants—which you will notice at other stalls throughout the Medina—are made with striped, plaid, and checked fabrics. They are comfortable, and a very stylish choice for both women and men to wear with a t-shirt or short caftan. Beware, the prices vary dramatically. Everything depends upon your <u>subtle</u> bargaining prowess, and the mood of the seller.

3. Fnaque Berbère

CASH ONLY ● DAILY

As you continue your walk, you'll notice that the Rue Mouassine makes a little jog before it straightens out again. In the crook of the jog is the book and newspaper kiosk Fnaque Berbère. The Fnaque sign says that it's the Premiere Librairie in Marrakech. This double entendre lets you know that not only is this hole-in-the-wall the best bookshop but it's also the first. Well, not the best anymore, but after seven decades in the same spot selling newspapers, Moroccan-themed books, maps, and postcards—all in limited supply—this institution deserves support and the right to be called the first. Besides, the kindly and smiling proprietor is hard to resist.

4. Khartit Mustapha

3 FHAL CHIDMI, RUE MOUASSINE ● Tel: 212 024 44 25 78
ALL CREDIT CARDS ● DAILY 8AM – 9PM

On the left side of the *rue,* find this rather large shop. Enter the shop and you'll feel sure that you've stumbled on the cave of an errant pirate. My, what booty! The rooms of this dusty place are chock-a-block filled with mother-of-pearl inlaid furniture, Orientalist paintings, silver Berber jewelry—both modern and antique, and hundreds,

maybe thousands, of semiprecious stones and beads arranged in dazzling color combinations on brass trays and in ceramic bowls. The stones and beads are sold by weight. Mustapha and his staff are exceedingly helpful without being pushy. They'll custom-make jewelry according to your desires. Khartit refers to a rhinoceros tusk. It's doubtful that you'll find one here these days—at least one hopes.

5. Aziz

CASH ONLY ● NO PHONE ● SHOP HOURS MUCH DEPEND ON THE MAN HIMSELF.

Aziz is the proprietor of a little shop a few doors away from Khartit Mustapha. The sign outside the shop is Aziz himself—quite possibly the chicest man in Marrakech. Dressed from head (a lilac knit cap) to toe (Concord grape babouches) in shades of purple, Aziz is typically

seen threading beads onto wire, as he has done for the past 35 years, to fashion his unique jewelry. Step inside his tiny shop and choose an antique silk scarf, a piece of ancient pottery, a piece of jewelry, either vintage Berber or an Aziz original.

6. Dar Cherifa

8 DERB CHERFA LAKBIR ● Tel: 212 024 42 64 63
CASH ONLY ● DAILY 9AM–7PM

You'll need to follow the directions on the map to get to this magnificent literary café and art gallery. Don't be daunted—with a few precise twists and turns, you're there. Duck into a rather innocuous-looking entrance and find yourself inside the oldest and one of the grandest riads—a traditional Moroccan home with a courtyard—in Marrakech. Once home to an imam who was a professor of religion, Dar Cherifa is now an oasis of calm within the noisy souks. Peruse the revolving exhibits of photos, paintings, and sculpture made by local and international artists—all for sale—then lay back on a comfortable divan, and order simply a refreshing beverage or lunch.

Check Dar Cherifa's website, www.marrakech-riads.net, for a schedule of events: lectures, concerts, poetry readings, etc., that will be happening while you're in Marrakech. Or email them: cafelitteraire@marrakech-riads.net.

7. Coffre Tissu

47 RUE MOUASSINE ☞ Tel: 212 024 44 31 63
SOME CREDIT CARDS; BEST TO HAVE CASH
DAILY 9AM – 7PM

When you leave Dar Cherifa, go back to the Rue Mouassine and continue walking northwards. You will come to a junction with Rue Sidi el Yamami. The restaurant **Bouganvillea** ✦ —offering tasty Moroccan and international-style salads, sandwiches, and pizzas all served in a riot-of-color, kitschy courtyard—will be on the opposite side of the street. Turn right, then take a quick left, to pick up the Rue Mouassine again. You'll know you're on the right track when you see the windows of

Coffre Tissu on the left crammed with piles of brightly-hued products. The shop is filled with highly colorful goods, from traditional striped cotton and silk fabrics made into bedspreads, pillow cases, and curtains, to equally colorful, striped raffia shoulder bags, slippers, and water-bottle and tea-glass holders. The style of raffia work found in this shop is unique and not as ubiquitous as the raffia-decorated and -trimmed bags, belts, and babouches found elsewhere.

Blaoui Abdelghani

146 RUE MOUASSINE ● NO PHONE
CASH ONLY ● DAILY 9 AM – 8 PM

O n the opposite side of the *rue*, just slightly north of Coffre Tissu, you'll recognize Blaoui's open shop when you see the stacks and stacks of antique pottery bowls, basins, jars, and tiles spilling out to the street from every direction. The majority of what you'll find are colorful, geometrically patterned ceramics from Fez in blue and white, and multicolored from Safi. All of the designs take their inspiration from nature whether a flower or tortoise. The wooden legal documents are perfect items to purchase. These cylindrical-shaped objects, covered with flowing Arabic script, are most often deeds to property and marriage proposals. They are unusual, lightweight and not too expensive.

9. Abdelhakim Keddabi

115 RUE MOUASSINE ● Tel: 212 70 21 68 48
SOME CREDIT CARDS ● DAILY 9AM – 8PM

Walking north, on the opposite side of the *rue* from Blaoui look for this closet of a shop with buttery soft lambskin bags and belts hanging just outside the front door. Keddabi's singular style is evident from the thin, wound silk shoulder straps and scallop-edged flaps on the bags. The belts have a large, oval, padded-leather buckle. Both items come in delicious, hard-to-resist colors. Imagine a raspberry pink bag slung across a black cashmere sweater, or a pale pink linen shirt cinched with a pistachio green belt.

10. Boutique La Douce

RUE MOUASSINE ● NO PHONE
SOME CREDIT CARDS ● DAILY 9AM – 8PM

A few shops to the north of Keddabi find this similarly-sized shop with similar goods made of different materials. La Douce carries a selection of sherbet-colored suede bags, babouches, and belts that are decorated with raffia embroidery. There's also a small selection of embroidered and bejeweled caftans.

Across the street from this shop find the refreshing **Café Arabe** ✦ . This Italian-owned restaurant serves both Italian and Moroccan dishes. Their indoor rooms are elegantly casual—their rooftop dining area is a treat at sunset.

11. Caravanserai

CASH ONLY ● DAILY 9AM – 9PM

As the Rue Mouassine ends, make a left turn onto the Rue Dar el Bacha. Start to look to the left and to the right for entrances into grand courtyards. These are the caravanserai and foundouks where

merchants and their burden-loaded camels came to rest after making the trek to the Marrakech oasis from the sub-Saharan regions. These days, under the aegis of UNESCO's program to preserve world cultural sites, these two caravanserai, in particular, have been beautifully restored and are now homes to sellers of made-in-Morocco goods, including carpets, tassels, chess sets, babouches, belts, bags, and shawls.

12. Tile Place

CASH ONLY ● NO PHONE ● DAILY 9 AM – 8 PM

n the left side, just past the caravanserai look for a hole in the wall, literally, with a cornice inlaid with yellow tiles. Peak inside to find a variety of tiles with chiseled designs of familiar Moroccan subjects: teapots, palm trees, tagine dishes, animals, fruit, etc. The painstaking work of slowly chipping away at a glazed tile until the design is

achieved results in an innocently chic object—incredibly poetic in its simplicity. Bargain if you dare—but these artisans are easily offended if the amount that you pay for their product isn't commensurate with the work they've put into it.

13. R. Bati

41 RUE DAR EL BACHA ● Tel: 212 044 44 44 92
SOME CREDIT CARDS ● DAILY 9AM – 8PM

urther up on the left find this charming antique shop. The owners are particularly proud of a nineteenth-century wedding dress embroidered with phrases from the Koran (it might still be there!), as well as their collection of vintage saddles. Also of interest are marble fountains, painted wooden ceilings from the eighteenth century which you can ship home to make your very own Moroccan riad, eighteenth- and nineteenth-century ceramics, and Moroccan-themed paintings both vintage and contemporary.

14. Khalid Art Gallery

14 RUE DAR EL BACHA ● Tel: 212 044 42 72 28
MOST CREDIT CARDS ● DAILY 9AM – 8PM

This "art" gallery, up the street on the right, is a super luxurious antique shop. The owner will proudly tell you that the young king of Morocco shops here. There is a wall of celebrity photos that prove it and it will leave you gaga as to who else frequents the gallery.

Among the embarrassment of riches don't overlook the antique, painted Berber doors, silk-embroidered decorative valances, incised copper and brass food warmers/servers, elaborately decorated wooden lanterns, delicate and sweetly painted blue-and-white basins, decorated vases made just to hold olives, carpets, antique clothing—and paintings, posters, and pottery galore. In addition Khalid has a good selection of mirrors that look just like they came from Murano—in fact the glass comes from Italy, but the end product is made in Morocco.

15. Zimroda

**18 RUE DAR EL BACHA ● NO PHONE ● SOME CREDIT CARDS
DAILY 9 AM – 8 PM**

A few doors away from Khalid, Zimroda specializes in modern and vintage jewelry. But jewelry is hardly the sum of the merchandise offered by the owner, and African kickball champion (of all interesting career combinations!), Ahmed Khattab. Certain very, very famous American movie stars—again, see the obligatory wall of photos—have found walking sticks with distinctive and unusual handles, painted doors, mirrors, paintings, metal boxes, special-occasion turquoise ceramic tagine dishes decorated with silver, and a nice collection of Judaica including menorahs and Sabbath wine cups, at this friendly shop.

16. Librairie Dar El Bacha

2 RUE DAR EL BACHA ☎ Tel: 212 024 39 19 73
WWW.DARELBACHA.COM ☎ SOME CREDIT CARDS. BRING CASH.
DAILY 9AM – 7PM

Find this small, modern, well-supplied bookstore specializing in books, reproduction vintage postcards, vintage Moroccan stamps and posters, a few doors away from Zimroda. They also carry maps, guidebooks, and, in particular, Moroccan cookbooks in English. One of the things that makes this shop so attractive to the traveler is that they sell the stamps that you need for your postcards.

You'll see the Dar el Bacha, the palace of the pasha, across the street from the bookshop—you might want to duck inside and have a look around—or you might prefer to continue shopping. Then cross the slightly wider street into the Rue Bab Doukkala. You'll pass a haphazard collection of petit taxis. Begin to keep your eyes peeled for a truly tiny tailor's shop, which you should recognize by the brightly colored caftans and djellabahs hanging in the window.

17. Ben Zouine Med Rida

RUE BAB DOUKKALA ● Tel: 212 024 38 50 56
CASH ONLY ● DAILY 9AM – 1PM AND 3PM – 7PM

The exceedingly talented, well-mannered tailor within will take your measurements, then proceed to make you a short or long caftan, a djellabah (like a caftan, but with a hood), a cape, or pants in the fabric of your choice with simple, or intricate, embroidery in three days—all the more reason for making this the FIRST walk of your stay!

18. Mustapha Blaoui

144 RUE BAB DOUKKALA ● Tel: 212 024 38 52 40
SOME CREDIT CARDS ● DAILY 9AM – 7:30PM

More or less next door to the tailor is M. Blaoui's warehouse of treasures. If you make only one stop while in Marrakech, this is the place. Look for the large, wooden, brass-studded, double doors, opened slightly, or not—there is no sign—but there is the number 144 hammered onto the door with brass studs. Knock for entry. The darling of every one of his customers, Mustapha's twinkling smile immediately puts you at ease, and when he lifts an eyebrow with a secret signal to one of his staff—within minutes a silver tray of glasses of tea, stuffed full with fresh mint appears and you are ready to shop! Oh, what choices. Early on Blaoui recognized the fashion for white pottery and made classic tagine dishes in all sizes, spice jars, and platters all in glazed white ceramic for his customers' pleasure. Cedar chests of drawers covered in brightly colored goatskin, decorated with complementary leather stitches and brass studs, are stacked to the very high ceiling. There are water-bottle holders made with a non-tarnishing metal alloy called mechour. There are mechour-topped clothes brushes and hands of Fatima (some decorated with six-pointed stars because until 40 years ago the Moroccan star had six points); lanterns; dowry chests from Rif, in the northern part of the country, decoratively painted with a mixture of pigeon droppings and herbs; Touareg

(the nomads of the Sahara desert) rugs from the southern Maghreb (Morocco and Algeria) tightly woven with split palm leaves and camel leather to make them impervious to the desert sand; and antique Berber babouches—just to mention a fraction of the inventory. If you stick

around long enough, you may spot a well-known French philosopher king, or the regal widow of an Italian automobile mogul slouching in one of Blaoui's comfortable armchairs enjoying a glass of sweet tea and conversation. Worldwide shipping available.

RIAD EMDI – **54** ARSET AOUZAL ● **Tel:** 212 65 99 58 75

his atelier of Frenchwoman Marie Dominique Jauzon is located down a few narrow streets not too far away from M. Blaoui. However, Madame Jauzon is not always in residence in Marrakech so it would be best to arrange an appointment with her (mdjauzon@wanadoo.fr). She would be happy to come meet you at Blaoui's or near the petit taxis where Rue Bab Doukkala meets Rue Dar el Bacha and escort you to her shop. It's worth the extra effort needed to arrange the visit—her spot-on sense of style comes from her background in the French fashion industry. Her short caftans made from Harris tweed, Glen plaid, and toile de Jouy prints on linen and cotton, silk, and Moroccan "cashmere," then decorated with embroidery and soutache in the classic Moroccan way, are stunning. Everything else in her studio—bags, babouches, brooches, and swimsuit covers—are designed by her. She carefully follows the manufacture of every piece that she sells, thereby assuring top-quality items.

Madame Jauzon can almost always be found in Marrakech around the Christmas and Easter holidays—as well as other times.

If you're so inclined, and still have some energy, after you've finished with these shopping suggestions, take a walk west on the Rue Bab Doukkala to the bab—the gate—where you will find yourself opposite the bus station. In the meantime you will have walked through a real neighborhood full of interesting, local shops. Near the gate there are vendors with their wares laid on the street, selling beautiful green glazed pottery. You can easily find a petit taxi at the bus station to take you back home.

20. Droguerie et Electricité Boutouil

90–91 RUE BOUTOUIL • Tel: 212 044 38 09 42

If you've found the ubiquitous blue at the Majorelle gardens irresistible, then before you walk out through the gate—Bab Doukkala—turn right and walk down the Rue Boutouil to number 90–91, where you'll find the Droguerie et Electricité Boutouil. The shop is the sole vendor of already-mixed Bleu Majorelle paint in the city. Buy the Astral brand, matte, because it's so heavily pigmented that you'll only need one coat to cover whatever you want to paint.

WALK № 2

• • ◉ • •

Bab Laksour, Rue Sidi El Yamami, Into the Souks

WALK Nº2

Yards   100   200

N
W   E
S

RUE FATIMA ZOHRA

RUE JEBEL LAKHDAR

Ensemble
Artisanal

● 1

● 2

7 ●   ● 8
    4 ●
    5
 RUE
6 ●

3 ●
Bab
Laksour

AVENUE MOHAMED V   RUE JEBEL LAKHDAR

1. Ensemble Artisanal

AVENUE MOHAMED V ● **Tel:** 212 044 38 67 58
ALL CREDIT CARDS ● DAILY 8:30AM–7:30PM

Walk or take a petit taxi to this cavernous mini-mall on the Avenue Mohamed V. The Ensemble is a government-sponsored crafts center where the artisans are hand-picked by committee and then given the seal of royal appointment—which results in nothing more than allowing the vendors to charge high, non-negotiable prices. Quickly peruse the merchandise, especially the metalwork. Make mental notes of what you like and continue shopping—you can always come back later.

2. Berrada

4 RUE JEBEL LAKDHAR ● **Tel:** 212 024 37 80 80
ALL CREDIT CARDS ● DAILY 9AM–12:30PM AND 3–7:30PM

Walk out of Ensemble Artisanal's doors on the Avenue Mohamed V side and turn left. Make another quick left on the Rue Jebel Lakhdar which almost immediately curves around to your left again. On the right side you will find, at number 4, the modern Moroccan home furnishings shop Berrada. Using traditional Moroccan methods for the crafts of ceramics, metalwork, and glasswork, the artisans employed by Berrada have created up-to-date tableware. Witness the eye-catching square dinner plates glazed in acid green, burgundy, and deep sky blue.

The handles of Berrada's signature flatware are decorated with multicolored glass beads, and their wineglasses are painted with Moorish-inspired flourishes.

3. Aachab Atlas

RUE SIDI EL YAMAMI ● **Tel:** 212 024 42 67 28
CASH PREFERRED ● DAILY 9AM–7:30PM

When you leave Berrada turn left, walk across the Rue Fatima Zohra and through the gate Bab Laksour, which will leave you on the Rue Sidi el Yamami (on some maps Yumani). On the left side of the *rue* you will immediately find the three centuries–old Aachab (pharmacy in Arabic) Atlas. Enter the door to find white-ceilinged, tile-walled and -floored rooms stocked with jars and canisters filled with herbs and spices. The knowledge-able staff will carefully explain the salubrious qualities of each item. Purchase a bottle of found-only-in-Morocco argan oil to stave off wrinkles or to soothe your arthritic joints (used in symphony with arnica oil), a jar of rose cream to soften your skin, musk oil to keep moths away, amber to discourage mosquitoes, and jasmine oil to perfume your home. This pharmacy will prescribe nigella seeds wrapped in a hanky to inhale to keep you from snoring, and poppy seed salve to guard against dry lips.

4. Kulchi

1 BIS RUE EL KSOUR ● Tel: 212 024 43 77 02/10
WWW.COMPTOIRDARNA.COM ● MOST CREDIT CARDS
DAILY 9:30AM–1PM AND 3–7:30PM

When you leave the pharmacy, turn left and walk a short distance to a right turn down the Rue el Ksour (it's a gentle incline)—you will see the sign for Kulchi on the left side. Kulchi is owner Florence Taranne's Medina outpost. She also owns the popular Le Comptoir—restaurant, club, and boutique—outside the walls, in Hivernage. Taranne's Kulchi is a sweet little shop with a selection of unique, one-of-a-kind clothing and housewares. Of particular interest are the stools that are, in fact, upholstered metal oil cans. Her take on the classic Moroccan pouf results in an interesting mix of patterned leather pieces—which could be called hip-hop for their almost rhythmical compositions. There are also the de rigueur designer's interpretation of caftans, jewelry, and babouches.

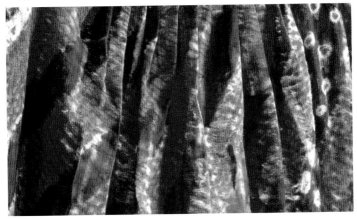

5. Chez Khayati

5 RUE EL KSOUR ● NO PHONE
SOME CREDIT CARDS; BRING CASH

You'll recognize Mustapha Khayati's place two doors down from Kulchi because the majority of his goods are on display outside his workroom/shop. M. Khayati is a master leather-worker and his ingenious

cushions, poufs, and babouches are proof of his talent. The poufs, both the traditional round shape, and his square, more modern version, are fashioned with geometric cuts of leather sewn together with outside stitching to create a pleasing patchwork effect. Khayati may keep the hours of his European neighbors—or he may stay open from 9am–7:30pm.

6. Kifkif

8 RUE EL KSOUR ● Tel: 212 061 08 20 41
WWW.KIFKIFBYSTEF.COM ● MOST CREDIT CARDS
DAILY 9:30AM–1PM AND 3–7:30PM

Just down the hill from Khayati find this delightful shop with the air of an old-fashioned dry goods store. The entrepreneurial owner, Stephanie Benetiere, has covered all the bases with her varied selection of personally-designed products. She says, more or less, that she combines "the Moroccan know-how" along with "personal and Western influences" to create her belts, bags, key rings, babies' and children's clothing, t-shirts, shawls, metallic leather poufs, embroidered tablecloths and napkins, rice or café au lait bowls and tea glasses hand-painted with traditional Moroccan motifs, leather jewelry or sewing boxes, leather-bound notebooks, and the shop's signature item, ceramic medallions printed with images from vintage Moroccan postcards strung on silk cords. The shop also carries multicolored, knit camels that are not only the perfect souvenir for your favorite child but a charity item too—half of the profits from the sale will be donated to the city's children's hospital.

7. Dar Bou Ziane

20–21 RUE SIDI EL YAMAMI ● Tel: 212 024 44 33 49
MOST CREDIT CARDS ● DAILY 9:30AM–1PM AND 3–7:30PM

After you leave KifKif, go back up the hill to Rue el Yamami—you will immediately recognize the entrance to this antique shop by its open, heavy wooden doors, and the brass monogram, DB, above the portal in graceful script. As you enter, steel yourself for very high prices, but know that the staff expects fierce bargaining from you. Dar Bou Ziane are known for their great selection of inlaid furniture. These stunning pieces—mostly from Meknes—are inlaid with mother-of-pearl and camel bone; some pieces are tinted with henna. There's a huge selection of decorated pottery, and of solid-colored turquoise, and some pieces of green pottery as well. Of particular interest are the wedding bells which are shown used as curtain tie backs. Find a good selection of Orientalist paintings as well.

Radi

20 RUE SIDI EL YAMAMI ● Tel: 212 044 44 39 96
CASH ONLY ● DAILY 9:30AM–7:30PM

Diagonally across the street from Dar bou Ziane (true, it's the same address—call it quirky city planning!), look for a door just cracked open. Peek inside—if you see stacks of metal plates and shelves filled with glasses, you're in the right place. Radi sells to the trade—but in true merchant style, he'll sell to whomever pays him. Just be discreet. The metal chargers, teapots, lanterns, and tea-glass holders are made with brass or the non-tarnishing metal alloy called mechour. Most of the glass items are made with Iraqi glass prized because of its durability.

After you leave Radi, continue walking eastward and you will soon find La Maison du Kaftan on your left. The house of caftans is comprised of two huge rooms. One room is for garments made with

high-quality fabrics: velvet, silk velvet, wool, cotton, and the brushed cotton known as Moroccan "cashmere." There are a great variety of colors, and color combinations in every fabric. There are caftans embroidered with thread that matches the cloth, and there are those decorated with complementary and contrasting threads. Of singular beauty is a rose-colored wool djellabah (a caftan with a hood) lined with blue and white stripped cotton. The second room is filled with pretty things, but at much lower prices. Don't be put off by the almost dreary display in this store—it remains a <u>must</u> for the fashionistas who pass through Marrakech. Take your time and carefully look through the racks—you'll be astounded at the treasures you'll find jammed between some rather dull things.

Ministero del Gusto

22 DERB AZZOUZ ● Tel: 212 024 42 64 55
EMAIL MINGUSTO@MENARA.MA ● SOME CREDIT CARDS
MONDAY THROUGH FRIDAY 9:30AM–12PM,
OR CALL FOR AN APPOINTMENT

As soon as you leave La Maison, start to look on the left side of the *rue* for an archway entrance to the narrow alley, Derb Azzouz. Follow it as it twists and turns for about a hundred feet until you find Ministero del Gusto on your left. Enter this fantastical gallery/store/performance space and be prepared to be thoroughly mesmerized by the clever use of the multistoried space by the Italian owners, designer/decorators Alessandra Lippini and Fabrizio Bizzari. Call this style Africa-revisited, mid-century Moroccan—whatever, it's just the kind of place that makes you feel as if you've been let in on a little secret. Everything's for sale, including a stash of vintage clothing. Don't you need an Emilio Pucci sunhat? The exhibitions change every three months.

94 MOUASSINE (ENTRANCE IS ON RUE SIDI EL YAMAMI)
Tel: 212 024 38 01 25 ● SOME CREDIT CARDS
DAILY 9:30AM–7:30PM

When you leave Ministero go back to the main drag, Rue Sidi el Yamami, turn left, pass the **Bouganvillea** ✦ restaurant on your left,
then look for this modern shop, trimmed in light colored wood,
across the way. Assouss Argane is devoted to selling products made with this
truly native-to-Morocco-only oil. As a matter of fact, argan trees grow in
the arid land that stretches between
Marrakech and the seaside town of Es-
saouira. The nuts grow on gnarly and
thorny trees which look prehistoric—
and are. The nuts are encased in green
flesh that makes them resemble olives.
It is a laborious task to remove the oil
from the nut, a job handled by women
only. The roads between Marrakech, Es-
saouira, and Agadir are dotted with
women's cooperatives dedicated to argan oil production. In its raw state, the
oil is used for cosmetics. Assouss carries
argan oil mixed with volcanic clay for
face masks, shampoo, soap, and creams
for all skin types. Some of the nuts are
toasted first and then the oil is extracted
for use in food. There are bowls of the
nuts displayed around the shop for the
curious.

12. Maktoub

128 RUE SIDI EL YAMAMI ● **Tel:** 212 024 44 54 06
SOME CREDIT CARDS ● DAILY 9:30AM–7:30 PM

Continue your walk east on the Rue Sidi el Yamami and look carefully on your left side for an ornate brass-decorated wooden door—it's opposite the landmark Fontaine Mouassine. Maktoub just opened in 2009, an enterprise of one of the brothers of the great Blaoui merchant family. Maktoub means "it is written" in Arabic and so it seems that it was written that this Blaoui frère return to his native city after living abroad for more than thirty years. His taste, honed by the fashions of faraway places, insinuates itself in his own line of clothing, a collection of vintage caftans, antique jewelry, and contemporary and vintage housewares galore, including exquisite, ancient wedding blankets. Enter the shop if only to view the extraordinary space made up of a string of connecting rooms.

13. Moro

When you exit Maktoub, look to your left—you should see a pale apricot-colored, two-story building standing perpendicular to the *rue*—there are leather bags sitting on the roof as parapet markers. Walk over and press the buzzer for Moro on the second floor. Someone will come downstairs to open the door for you. As soon as you climb the stairs to this glorious emporium, rest a second and catch your breath. You'll need to be fully aware as you peruse Moro's products. Check out the beautiful white cotton bibs and booties, lovingly quilted by ladies from Fez. There are brightly striped hammam

(bath) towels from Tangier, quilts, ballerina-style babouches, caftans—newly made but with vintage fabrics, short suede caftans for both men and women, silk belts with Venetian glass buckles, handsomely stitched leather pouches that hold pretty little coffee spoons with striped ceramic handles, ditto for salad turners, and wool tassels—that you could use to decorate a curtain tie-back or a drawer key. There are deliciously-scented handmade soaps that are true to their original ingredients—rose, mint, and orange flower—and crocheted wool-covered bottles of argan-oil-and-eucalyptus soap. Be sure to look down at the floor that you walk on—it's made of leather. Ah, what inspiration.

(The sign says 9:30am–12:30pm and 2–7pm; however, they seem to keep their own hours.)

14. Magasin Berbère

41 SOUK LABBADINE ● NO PHONE
SOME CREDIT CARDS ● DAILY 9:30 AM–7:30 PM

When you walk out of Moro, turn right then a quick right again under an archway that will lead you into the souks. As you follow the gently curving street, keep a lookout on your right for this shop. The window will be loaded with vintage teapots. Inside there is an unusually good selection of antique and modern Berber silver rings, some set with amber or lapis lazuli. There are modern necklaces made with vintage beads, and necklaces made with carved and whole shells. The goods are topnotch at this place, so it's a bit pricey. Bargain carefully. The owner is accommodating.

15. Masrour Abdellah

53 SOUK LABBADINE ● NO PHONE
CASH ONLY ● DAILY 9:30 AM–7:30 PM

Stay to the right when you leave Magasin Berbère and soon you will come upon the open-air workplace/shop of the dyer and felted goods fabricator Masrour Abdellah. Here is a dazzling display of brightly-colored goods: bags, hats, necklaces made with felted beads, and lovely flower-shaped objects with wired stems. Twist the flower into your hair, or buy a bunch to stand in a beautiful piece of Moroccan pottery. Once you've purchased the flowers, you will be invited to choose a felted bead to place in the center of the petals.

16. L'Art Touareg – Chez Latif

21 SOUK DES TEINTEURS ● Tel: 212 024 39 07 28
SOME CREDIT CARDS ● DAILY 9:30AM–7:30PM

Keep walking to the right and soon you will see the rather formal-looking (proper shop windows trimmed in rich brown wood) façade of Chez Latif. You've just been to the Berber place and now you can shop at the Touaregs'. The Touaregs are nomadic people from the central Saharan area of North Africa—they are descended from the Berbers. Chez Latif carries many of the same products as Magasin Berbère. The necklaces at Chez Latif tend to be more ornate, and many are made with coral beads and branches. They are gorgeous. There are antique teapots—look for the very collectible teapots with eagle finials on the lid—this will tell you that they are Berber—not like the more easily found plain finials that are Arab. Discover the nice collection of antique Berber babouches.

L'Art du Bain

13 SOUK EL LBADINE (LABBADINE)
Tel: 212 067 49 16 10 ● SOME CREDIT CARDS
DAILY 9:30AM–1PM AND 3–7:30PM (HOURS ARE VARIABLE)

Keep walking to your right after you leave Chez Latif. You'll notice that the street widens into a kind of village square—L'Art du Bain will be on the right in a somewhat modern-looking space. Owners Elsa and Youssef Maanaoui have created a remarkable business with their great variety of handmade soaps in many shapes, sizes, and fragrances. Their unique soap dishes are made with mechour, the ubiquitous, non-tarnishing metal. They will happily fill a gift basket with a selection of their products. Make sure that they include one of their most unique items, a terra cotta trough made to fit on a light bulb. Fill the trough with one of L'Art du Bain's essential oils, say rose or jasmine—as the light bulb shines your room will become a garden in bloom.

18.
+ Michi

19–21 SOUK LAKCHACHBIA ● Tel: 212 061 86 44 07
WWW.MICHI-MOROCCO.COM ● SOME CREDIT CARDS
DAILY 9:30AM–7:30PM

When you leave L'Art du Bain, turn right and walk until you come to a junction, then turn left. Keep your eyes peeled for this adorable little shop on the left. + Michi is owned by a Japanese-Moroccan couple. There's no denying the combined esthetic. + Michi's very original babouches are sought after—if you like what you see buy them on the spot—in this place "he who hesitates is lost" for sure. There are bien choisi old things—there are things made to look old like the wire tea-glass carriers. There are shopping bags made with recycled plastic grain sacks, beautifully carved wooden spoons and forks with their own carrying cases made with recycled materials; there are Berber-style geometric patterned rag rugs, tasseled shoe horns, and articles of clothing elaborately trimmed by skilled Moroccan embroiderers using the + Michi team's designs.

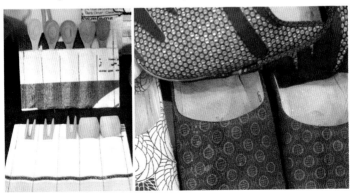

CASH ONLY ● DAILY 9AM–7:30 PM

When you leave + Michi walk to your left or to your right—look for an opening to the straw market which is in back of the block where + Michi stands. You'll be able to see stacks of straw products spilling out of little shops as you look down the lane. Walk into the compact straw souk. There's no one seller recommended over another—it would come as no surprise to realize that all the sellers are related. Some places are unattended, so if you want service just find a shop with a keeper and ask for his attention. There are terrific hats, bags in a wide variety of shapes and sizes, mats, baskets, mineral water covers, tea glass covers—and most interesting of all, straw baskets woven to look like tagine dishes. These baskets with their conical-shaped lids come in a variety of sizes, from tiny to grand. The tiny ones would be perfect set on a table as individual bread baskets. The large ones make a good place to store onions.

20. Création et Passementerie

2 SOUK EL KIMAKHINE ● **Tel:** 212 024 44 04 98
SOME CREDIT CARDS
DAILY 9:30AM–7:30PM, MAY CLOSE AT MIDDAY

This is a tricky little trip. After you leave the straw souk come back out onto the main drag. Walk to your left away from + Michi—when you come to a diagonal cross street make a left turn then a quick right—at this point look for a right turn onto the musical instruments Souk Kimakhine.

Just on your right find this two-story notions and trim shop. Upstairs is where you want to be. There's an enormous selection of silk tassels in every color and color combination imaginable, sized from tiny to gigantic. Buy the tassels neat or attached to a shoehorn or key chain. There are chains of crocheted beads; buy them neat to use as a window accent or a belt—or already made-up into a necklace. There are shawls, and babouches covered in sequins and made of striped fabrics or raffia-adorned leather, ballerina babouches, and flip-flops. But the real "get" are the curtain tie-backs that look like growths from a tropical sea—or extra-terrestrial creatures. The splendidly-colored, crocheted orbs have contrasting-colored twisted appendages leaping out from all around. They are attached to a corded loop.

Walk out of Création the same way that you came in, then turn right when you come to the main street. Walk along the street and keep your eyes peeled for a left turn into the Souk Cherifa. Almost immediately you'll find the entrance for the delightfully eccentric **Terrasse des Épices** ✦. Go upstairs, sit down, order a snack from their menu of local specialties or a refreshing beverage, and take in the roof-top views. You deserve a break. When you leave the Terrasse go back out the way you came in, turn left and you'll be on Rue Dar el Bacha. Follow it until you come to the gathering of petit taxis — one will take you home.

WALK № 3

• • ● • •

Place Bab Fteuh, Rue Semmarine, Into the Souks

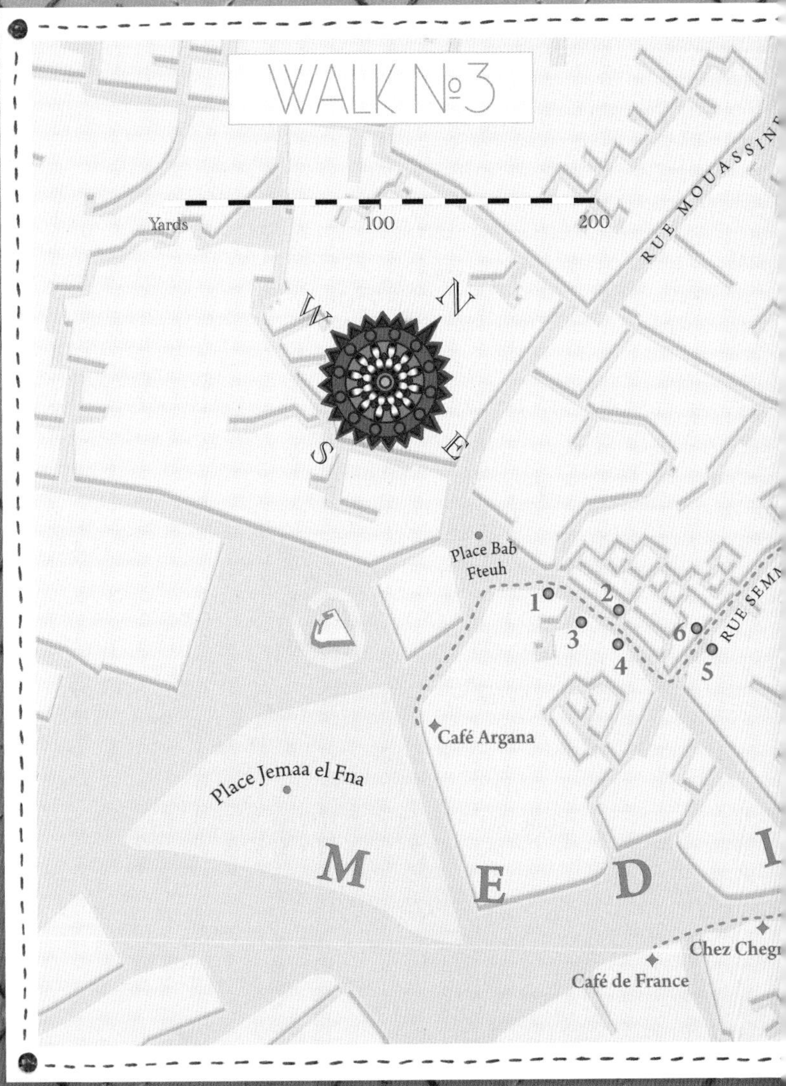

WALK N°3

Yards   100   200

RUE MOUASSINE

N
W   E
S

Place Bab
Fteuh

1
2
3
4
6
5

RUE SEMA

Café Argana

Place Jemaa el Fna

M   E   D   I

Chez Chegr

Café de France

Chez Mohamed

S O U K S

13

12

10

9

SOUK   EL   KEBIR

7

8

11

Café des Épices

Place Rahba Kdima

14

A

15

RUE RAHBA EL BIADYNE

N

BACHI   16

1. Akbar Delights

PLACE BAB FTEUH ✦ **Tel: 212 071 66 13 07**
WWW.AKBARDELIGHTS.COM ✦ MOST CREDIT CARDS
9:30AM–7:30PM; CLOSED MONDAY

Akbar Delights has a showroom in Gueliz at 42C Rue de la Liberté, 1st floor, apt. 47 (use the phone number above to make an appointment); the address will be pointed out on Walk 6 (page 195).

Just as you did for Walk 1, use the **Café Argana** ✦ as your start-off point. Go around the left side of the café into Place Bab Fteuh. Immediately look for Akbar Delights on your right. It's a tiny, tiny place set back a bit from the street. The shop is so small that Abdellah, who has worked at Akbar sinced it opened in 2004, stays outside to perform his dual tasks of refolding the merchandise after it's been tried, and packaging purchased items. Oh, and the ever-smiling Abdellah has a little side business—sometimes he sells rubber snakes, and other times Chinese toys. It's another way to recognize the shop. Consider yourself lucky if one of the owners and the designer, Yann Dobry, is in town and at the shop. The charming Frenchman Mr. Do-

bry is a facile raconteur in several languages. He designs all the merchandise and oversees its production in India (Akbar, a sixteenth-century Mughal, was considered the greatest of Indian rulers). The jewel-encrusted, sequin-adorned, gold-embroidered, paisley or ikat-printed fabric with soutache-trim caftans, kurtas (short caftans) and pillows will take your breath away. The purses and handbags are unique. Think ahead, and grab one right away for your next formal occasion, or simply as an accessory for a plain caftan. There are embroidered caps, necklaces and bracelets, and a nice selection of Moroccan-themed books. Lots of stuff for a small space.

2. Teapots and Tea Glasses Shops

PLACE BAB FTEUH ● CASH

lmost directly across the way from Akbar, you'll see a group of shops selling teapots and tea glasses. It would be well worth your while to take note of them. If you don't find what you like as you travel around, you can always return to this very convenient area to shop.

Back on the Akbar side of the *place* look for two things: a kind of dark entrance to what seems to be an antiques mini-mall, and a rusty number (37). There are in fact two separate antiques' (or old things, depending on your definition) courtyards right near each other. They are both housed in dilapidated foundouks. The one with the dark passageway comes first and it's the more interesting of the two courtyards. Walk past the little shops out into the open space. There are mountainous jumbles of stuff: lots

of sub-Saharan sculpture and masks, jugs, pottery, cooking equipment, textiles, and items made with copper and brass. Search for wooden mugs used for drinking water in the desert, and zigzag-patterned baskets—the ones with handles are used for sugar, and the ones with conical lids are used for bread. Check out the upstairs rooms. Treasures abound. Bargaining is a must. You'll constantly be courted by the sellers. Wave them away until you're ready. The second courtyard at number 37 has some of the same selections, but less variety.

5. Au Fil d'Or

10 SOUK SEMMARINE ● Tel: 212 024 44 59 19
ALL CREDIT CARDS EXCEPT AMEX
9AM–1PM AND 2:30–7:30 PM; CLOSED FRIDAY

After you leave the antiques courtyard, turn right and walk until you arrive at a junction—turn left onto the Rue Semmarine (Smarine on some maps). Almost immediately you will come upon Au Fil d'Or on your right. The shop is easily identified by its simple, classic window displays of exquisitely tailored caftans and buttery soft suede babouches in solid colors—plain and to the point. Enter the small shop and have a look at the upstairs stock but know that downstairs is where the interesting selection is housed. Make your way down through a trap door and a somewhat treacherous stair. There find the caftans, djellabahs, and men's "undershirts" upon which Au Fil d'Or has rightly made their international

reputation. There are caftans made of raw silk, and velvet too, covered with intricate gold embroidery; wool djellabahs; short jackets made with Moroccan "cashmere"—it's said that Au Fil d'Or coined the phrase—and covered with embroidery; men's undershirts made of silky-soft cotton, and of linen with hand-stitched collars—these are the shirts that men wear under their caftans. They come in short and long versions—short is actually three-quarters length. Au Fil d'Or will make everything to size and will ship.

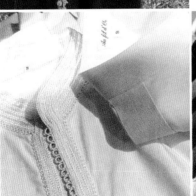

6. El Abidi Nasser Eddine

9 SOUK SEMMARINE ● **Tel:** 212 024 44 10 66
ALL CREDIT CARDS ● DAILY 9AM–8PM

Directly across the *rue* from Au Fil d'Or find this long established jewelry shop. There is both antique jewelry and modern jewelry made with antique materials. The helpful staff speaks multiple languages. They go out of their way to explain to the customer the provenance of each piece and how it's made. They will work with you to design something specific to your taste using Berber motifs. They also provide quite a unique service. They urge their customers to stay in contact with them and to keep their receipts. If, later on you decide that you've tired of your purchase, El Abidi Nasser Eddine will exchange it for something new. They also carry some small objects such as inkwells and perfume bottles.

Leave the jewelry shop and turn left. You'll be walking a bit before you come to this woodworking shop on the left. Rue Semmarine will widen and you'll pass textile shops and shops selling cheap clothing. Of interest along the way are the candy vendors selling pastel-colored nougats filled with almonds, or coconut macaroons that melt in your mouth—and the occasional seller of fezzes. At some point the Rue Semmarine becomes Souk El Kebir. You may smell the fresh wood shavings before you reach this sliver of a shop. It's located at a corner of a junction with a "major" left-turning street. Omar Siham, owner of L'Art du Bois, keeps a very active workshop in the rear of his store. All his products are made with orange wood. Among the many products, of particular interest are the molds (used for butter, cheese, or chocolate), every shape and size spoons and forks, little serving dishes, salad servers, citrus juicers, honey dippers, and wooden scissors.

8. Abdel Ilah Bennis

little bit past L'Art du Bois on the right is M. Bennis's stall. You'll know you're in the right place when you see a wall of color made of brightly-colored bags with tassels and elaborate embroidery in a contrasting color—especially delicious is a lavender bag with tangerine embroidery, and a cerulean blue bag with cherry red embroidery. So completely Yves St. Laurent!

These bags are among the defining goods of your Moroccan shopping experience. M. Bennis is a hard bargainer, but if you buy several bags—and you should—he'll make you a nice price.

9. Marrakech Rafia

iagonally across the way from M. Bennis find this stall, chock-a-block filled with leather goods decorated with raffia embroidery. There are shoulder bags in all sizes, knapsacks, babouches, belts, and poufs. Some are made with soft

leather, others with suede. All have a raffia-embroidered decoration. And there's something quite new: plaited-palm, bucket-shaped shopping bags covered in a jungle of raffia flowers.

10. Makchad Ahmed

129 SOUK EL KEBIR ● NO PHONE
CASH ONLY ● DAILY 9:30AM–8PM

Find this leather goods stall a few doors away from Marrakech Rafia. The sleek striped fabric and leather desktop accessories are to be considered. There are soft, cloth-covered notebooks, and suede ones too in a rainbow choice of colors. There are hardcover leather and suede notebooks as well. The cloth-covered, drum-

shaped boxes with faux-quilted leather tops in small or large are excellent gift options for the person whom you can never quite figure out.

11. Fashion Stoor

228 SOUK EL KEBIR ● NO PHONE
CASH ● DAILY 9:30AM–8PM

It's difficult to miss this crammed-to-the-rafters stall across the street from Ahmed. There's a lot of product here. Sift through the goods; you're bound to find just the right thing among the overnight bags. Some are carpet (kilim) bags (they sell whole rugs too); some are Gladstone bags, the kind that Holden Caulfield would happily carry to prep school; some are duffel bags; and there are shoulder bags, backpacks, poufs, and pillows.

12. Boutique Touil

149 SOUK EL KEBIR ● *Tel:* 212 044 42 66 95
CASH ● DAILY 9:30AM–8PM

Back on the other side of the street, find this pocket stall. You will be drawn in by the richly-colored products. The envelope leather handbags are very chic. The top-stitched, square poufs, in colors as tempting as aquamarine and persimmon, are hard to ignore. There are woven leather belts, and belts with metal decorations. There are leather totes—in a variety of colors—and knapsacks.

13.
Hassan Makchad

161 SOUK EL KEBIR ❖ **Tel:** 212 070 72 52 84
CASH ❖ DAILY 9:30AM–8PM

A few openings away from Touil, find the stall of another Makchad. His offerings are every bit as sophisticated as his relative's just a few steps away. Fortunately for the shopper the same high-quality workmanship is in evidence, but the selection varies. Hassan's drum-shaped leather boxes are covered with ruched leather and they come in true, emphatic colors like fuchsia and gold coin yellow. There are leather notebooks covered in gold-embossed designs and leather frames.

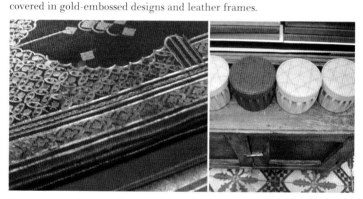

Now, here's where you have a choice. You can go further into the souks with the express goal of finding the most delicious street food—bar none. **Chez Mohamed** ✦ is found by continuing your journey to the left as you leave Hassan. Look for a gentle left turn. After you turn, keep an eye out for two things: one will be smoke mixed with the mouthwatering smell of grilling meat, and the other will be the façade of

Mohamed's kitchen, painted cerulean blue with dabs of white. Make your order as soon as you arrive. There will be a wait as Mohamed is it. He's the show. There are tiny tables, and equally tiny stools set up along the street in front of obliging merchants—and obvious fans of Mohamed. The souk that you've entered is the metalworkers'. Have a look around while you wait for your barbecued baby lamb chops, beef en brochettes, the spicy Moroccan sausage merquez, fresh herb omelettes, and chopped salad. Or, you can turn right after you leave Hassan and walk back as far as L'Art du Bois (you'll be coming back

this way to continue this walk even if you don't go to Chez Mohamed) and look for an opening just across from the shop—it will be on your left. Go through this narrow-ish passageway until it opens into the grand

Place Rahba Kdima. On your left find **Café des Epices** ✦ . This is the even more casual version of the same-owner Terrasse des Epices. Find refreshing drinks, great sandwiches, and wonderful views of the *place* from the second- and third-story rooms. After you leave the café, walk through the *place*, populated with all sorts of vendors, most notably those selling the knit skullcaps worn by Moroccan men, and more modern straw fedoras. When you're on the opposite side of the *place*, you should be in front of the open-air Herboriste Avicenne.

14. Herboriste Avicenne

172–174 PLACE RAHBA KDIMA ✿ NO PHONE
CASH ✿ DAILY 9:30AM–7:30PM

This natural plant pharmacy has been in business, in this spot, since the mid-nineteenth century. Here you will find a barrel of a tar-like substance which is actually soap—*savon beldi*. This ancient-formula soap is made almost entirely with olive oil, and a little argan oil. The idea is to rub the soap onto to your warm, moist body—leave it on for a few minutes and then scrub it off with a sandpaper-like mitt, or a corrugated terra cotta disk with a crochet covering—both for sale here. Look for dried fennel blossoms—twist the pod and let the seeds fall out, make an infusion with them, and you have a tonic for diabetes. Make an infusion with dried rose blossoms to cure constipation. A drop or two of nigella-seed oil will help soothe a delicate stomach. There are dried lizards that are ground, mixed with other ingredients, then used to cure more abstract maladies such as broken hearts. There's kohl to apply to the inside of your eyes to make them sparkle with mystery, and stencils to make it easy for you to apply henna tattoos on your hands, wrists, and ankles.

15. Art Ouazarzate

15 RUE RAHBA KDIMA (WHICH IS ACTUALLY
RUE RAHB EL BIADYNE) ● **Tel:** 212 012 14 89 63
SOME CREDIT CARDS ● DAILY 9 AM–8 PM

When you leave the *herboriste*, turn right, walk to the Rue Rahb el Biadyne and make another right turn. Almost immediately you'll see Art Ouazarzate to your right. This place calls itself a home decorations and accessories shop, but its real claim to fame is its rugs. They are marvelous. One of Art Ouazarzate's specialties is knotted leather rugs which they will make to order in any size and color combination. There are printed leather rugs and patchwork goatskin rugs. There are cotton Berber rugs in geometric patterns and ones in symphonies of fading solid colors. There are rugs with crocheted details. And, yes, there are accessories too: spectacular woven suede blankets and striped fabrics in wool, cotton, or linen that can be used to make curtains or bedspreads. There are the most fanciful bags made with heavy striped Berber cotton, lined with leather, heavily embroidered on the outside, with an antique, beaded, silk belt as the shoulder strap. This is the kind of place where the staff will invite you to sit down, and will serve you mint tea while they bring their wares to you. Perfectly civilized.

El Hyani Famille

Turn right when you leave Art Ouazarzate. You'll be walking through the
souk for a bit before you come upon
this next shop. Rue Rahb el Biadyne jogs
to the right, then quickly to the left—
El Hyani Famille will be on the left at the
point of a junction with Rue Dabachi. Almost everything in this pocket shop is
folded away in cases and drawers. It will be
brought out for your inspection upon
request. The original owners of the shop
made the heavily embroidered and bejeweled vests that were part of Yves St. Laurent's Moroccan-inspired collection. You
can still find products that recall that
collection as well as terrific caftans made
with nubby cotton, silk, and wool, and
earth-toned wool djellabahs perfect for
fending off the chill of the desert winter.

There's an original collection of belts
made with gold leather, velvet, and en-
crusted with cowrie shells. Don't let the
modest surroundings fool you—this place
is expensive. Their credit card policy is
capricious to say the least. The answer is
yes—sometimes—it all depends on your
total purchase!

At this point make your way back to the main square, the Jemaa el Fna. Leave Hyani—without making a sharp left, walk a little to the left then straight ahead—bear to your left and you'll be in the *place*, at the opposite end of your starting-off point. To your left find the restaurant **Chez Chegrouni** ✦ . Make a note. This place serves very tasty food at very affordable prices. Their menu includes both Moroccan— an amazing chicken and green olive tagine, and French bistro-style food—poulet et frites. Continue walking straight ahead and soon you'll come to the renowned **Café de France** ✦ . Toute le monde converges on the terraces of this café every evening to sip freshly squeezed orange juice or mint tea and watch the sun set over the Atlas Mountains.

WALK № 4

Rue Riad Zitoun El Jedid
to the Mellah

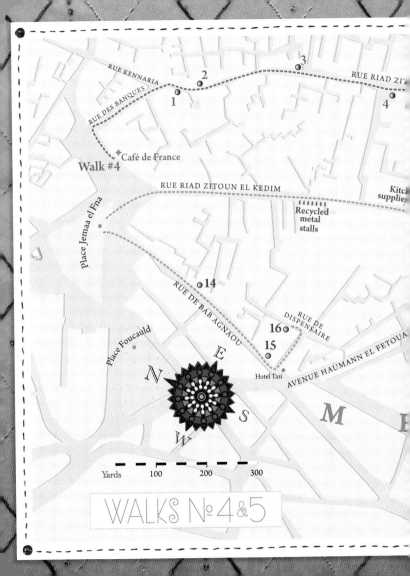

RUE KENNARIA

RUE RIAD ZIT

RUE DES BANQUES

2

3

1

4

♦ Café de France

Walk #4

RUE RIAD ZITOUN EL KEDIM

Kitc
supplie

Recycled
metal
stalls

Place Jemaa el Fna

14

RUE DE BAB AGNAOU

RUE DE
DISPENSAIRE

16

15

Place Foucauld

Hotel Tazi

AVENUE HAUMANN EL FETOUA

M

E

N

S

W

Yards   100   200   300

WALKS №4&5

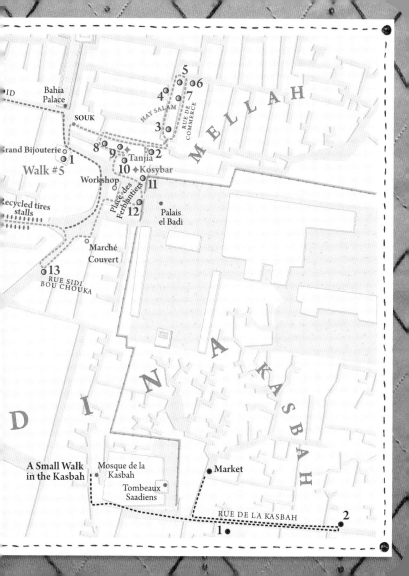

ID

Bahia
Palace

SOUK

Grand Bijouterie

Walk #5

1

8 **9**

2

Tanjia

10 ◆Kosybar

Workshop

11

Recycled tires
stalls

12

◆ Palais
el Badi

Marché
Couvert

13

RUE SIDI
BOU CHOUKA

5

4 **6**

7

HAY SALAM

RUE DE
COMMERCE

3

M E L L A H

Place des Ferblantiers

**A Small Walk
in the Kasbah**

Mosque de la
Kasbah

Tombeaux
Saadiens

● Market

RUE DE LA KASBAH

1 ●

2

M E D I N A

K A S B A H

Walks 4 and 5 can be easily combined. Logic dictates that these two walks that explore the southeastern part of the Medina be made together. Apart from the fact that you'll be walking in the same direction anyway—the shops and sights that you'll be encountering along the way are of great variety and contrast assuring a truly exhilarating shopping experience. However, if it appears to be more than you care to tackle at one go—the walks easily divide into two.

Begin Walk 4 at the **Café de France** ✦. You might want to down a fortifying café au lait before taking off. If you're facing the café, walk a few steps to your left and turn down the Rue des Banques. Keep to your right as the Rue des Banques very quickly becomes the Rue Riad Zitoun el Jedid.

1. Warda La Mouche

RUE KENNARIA ❧ Tel: 212 024 38 90 63
CREDIT CARDS ❧ DAILY 9:30AM–9PM

The shop calls its address Rue Kennaria which is the same as Rue Riad Zitoun el Jedid at this point (they merge at Rue des Banques). Warda La Mouche will be on your right, a few steps down the *rue*. This shop, whose name means "Rose the fly," has goods inside that justify its whimsical appellation. The French owner and her Moroccan husband—who designs the goods—call their style, non-traditional Moroccan. There are brightly-colored t-shirts covered with

embroidery, raffia shopping- and handbags decorated with ball fringe and other decorator's trim, velvet-flocked babouches and ones made of heavy cotton printed with crayon-colored flowers, and embroidered sailor's blouses. Here, you will find the ubiquitous caftan made with non-intuitive fabrics. There is a fine selection of men's items.

2. Bazar du Musée

38 RUE RIAD ZITOUN EL JEDID ● *Tel:* 212 071 84 26 28
SOME CREDIT CARDS ● DAILY 9:30AM–8PM

F urther down on the left is this shop selling every design, color, shape, and size of tea glasses that you could possibly imagine. Find a few useful tea glass accessories like brightly-colored raffia coasters and holders.

3. Jamade

RUE RIAD ZITOUN EL JEDID – 1 PLACE DOUR GRAOUA
Tel: 212 024 42 90 42 ● WWW.HOTELRIADCELIA.COM
SOME CREDIT CARDS ● DAILY 9:30AM–8PM

tay on the same side of the street as Bazar du Musée. Jamade will be easy to identify because it's set back off the street in quite a modern space. Step onto the shop's grape jelly-colored floor and you'll realize,

right away, that just about everything inside this shop that specializes in contemporary ceramics is modern. Jamade's artisans were the first group to modernize Moroccan pottery (according to them!) without completely abandoning traditional Moroccan forms. Their sleekly shaped teapots, vases, tagine and other covered serving dishes in muted vegetable colors—eggplant, pumpkin, zucchini, etc.—are kind of a relief for the eyes after looking at overwhelming amounts of vintage pottery. The shop carries other products by local designers including handmade shopping and cosmetic bags, coasters embroidered with Berber motifs from Tigmi (a women's cooperative), and jewelry.

4. El Idrissi

196 RIAD ZITOUN EL JEDID ● NO PHONE
CASH ONLY ● 9:30AM–8PM; CLOSED FRIDAY AFTERNOON

Across the way and down the street from Jamade, find the corner-of-a-cul-de-sac shop of this *zelliguer* – one who

cuts tiles. Mustapha—the kind, calm, very religious man – sits in the center of his workspace/shop and taps designs into glazed ceramic tiles. His work includes verses from the Koran in Arabesque script, animals, everyday objects such as bread (identified as *pain*), signs for the W.C. and the *bain*, bath. He also carries numbered ceramic tiles.

5. Kasbek

216 RUE RIAD ZITOUN EL JEDID
KAS **212 063 77 56 90** ● BEK **212 069 95 20 30**
SOME CREDIT CARDS ● DAILY **10**AM–**7**PM

Stay on the right side of the *rue* and you will soon find this shop owned by two Australian women, Cassie and Rebecca. The caftans, which are the calling card of the shop, are made with vintage caftans which have been re-cut to become more figure flattering—narrower on the top, per-

haps a higher slit up the leg—you know. There are caftans made from scratch with the signature, tie-dyed fabrics from Mauritania—these garments come with matching drawstring bags. These Aussie women have their fingers on the pulse of what the young, hip traveler to Marrakech wants. They offer just the right accessories to wear with their caftans; contemporary silver jewelry, chunky necklaces made with ceramic beads and shells, woven silver handbags, and metallic leather babouches and sandals.

When you leave Kasbek, continue walking to your right. Soon you will come to the entrance, on your left, for the Bahia Palace. Here's what Edith Wharton, in her illuminating travelogue, In Morocco, had to say about the Bahia Palace: "Whoever would understand Marrakech must begin by mounting at sunset to the roof of the Bahia.

Outspread below lies the oasis-city of the south, flat and vast as the great nomad camp it really is, its low roofs extending on all sides to a belt of blue palms ringed with desert."

You probably won't be at the palace at sunset; however, a side trip to visit the grounds and the interior, much deteriorated since Wharton's visit, will put everything you've seen and are about to see into perspective.

Leave the palace and make your decision whether to loop around and return to the main Place Jmaa el Fna via the Rue Riad Zitoun el Kedim or continue further into the Mellah, on Walk 5.

WALK № 5

• • • • •

The Mellah Back Through Rue Riad Zitoun El Kedim

Map page 124

The Mellah, the old Jewish quarter of Marrakech, is a neighborhood all its own. It's calmer, quieter, and has a lighter spirit than the more densely populated area of the souks. Because of the variety and uniqueness of the stores, the Mellah is a shopping destination for locals, foreign residents, and tourists. Not only is there evidence of the once thriving Jewish population in Marrakech—approximately 36,000 at the beginning of the twentieth century, now hovering around 260—in the signs with Hebrew lettering, the occasional Star of David above doorways, and the remains of the walls that at one time divided the area from the rest of the Medina, but also in the shops themselves that are direct descendants of the Jewish trades: trimmings— especially crocheted buttons, glassworks, metalworkers—evident in numerous hardware stores and in the jewelry souk, and the well-stocked Marché Couvert—also

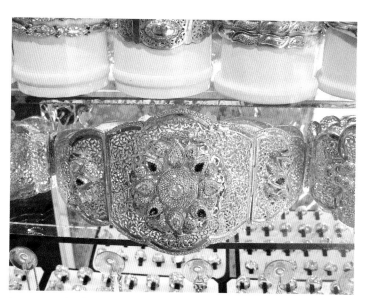

known as the Jewish Market. One thing to know: unlike the more centrally located souks that are open seven days a week, this neighborhood respects the traditional Muslim Sabbath and most of the shops are closed on Fridays, or at least for the afternoon. So, plan these walks accordingly.

When you leave the Bahia Palace, walk straight ahead and you will soon notice the arched entrance to the Grand Bijouterie, the jewelry souk. Walk in and make the rounds of the many tiny shops selling ornate gold jewelry: jewel-encrusted bracelets and belts, bangles, and necklaces. The item to seriously consider is to be found in the rear-corner shop, Al Wady Abdelkarim.

1. Al Wady Abdelkarim

26 BIJOUTERIE DE L'ORO ● *Tel:* 212 070 74 69 19
SOME CREDIT CARDS ● 9:30AM–1PM AND 3–7:30PM;
CLOSED FRIDAY AFTERNOON

In addition to the aforementioned items Al Wady has a nice selection of the gold-coin earrings that are the everyday, chosen accessory for many Moroccan women. These drop earrings have a gold French sou attached to half an orb or a gold-framed ruby. They could make a genuine Moroccan souvenir—something that the locals buy for themselves—and a bit of a change from all the silver and beaded items that you've been seeing as you make the rounds.

When you leave the Grand Bijouterie, go out the same way you came in—look across the rather busy intersection to your right – you'll see the entrance to a major souk. Go under the archway and walk until you come to a junction. Turn right into a little cul-de-sac.

NUMBER 29 BOUTIQUE ● Tel: 212 024 38 19 20
CASH ● 9:30AM–7:30PM; CLOSED FRIDAY AFTERNOON

Opposite the entrance find this trimmings shop—one of the city's most popular. Don't be surprised if you find yourself jockeying for position near a very blonde French matron looking for just the right curtain tieback for her new villa in the Palmerie, or a sleekly handsome young Moroccan who has all of a sudden become Marrakech's most sought-after decorator searching for the same. Everyone has identical, exciting choices from gigantic tassels anchored with silver caps, to tassels that are fanciful bunches of crocheted buttons. If instead, you prefer to pick up some smaller gift items there are tasseled bookmarks, key rings, and shoehorns; there are silk-wrapped and decorated pens; and there are small-enough-for-a-lipstick-keys-and-a-$50-bill crocheted bags; and metal bags with knotted cord straps. As a matter of fact, buy some of these items in multiples. They make perfect party favors.

3. Idbelkacem Mohamad

28 HAY SALAM • **Tel:** 212 066 30 90 97
CASH • 9AM–7:30PM; CLOSED FRIDAY AFTERNOON

Walk back out to the main drag, turn right, then quickly left into a very busy shopping area. Very soon, on the right, you'll recognize this singular shop, among the many, by the colorful bags hanging from the entranceway. They're raffia bags that have been covered with brightly colored, vintage, heavy cotton. The bags are adorned with beads and shells and the rope-like handles are made with multicolored beads. The shop has other small items—but the bags are the reason to stop here.

Benyahya Khalid

173 HAY SALAM ● Tel: 212 044 37 69 15
CASH ● 9 AM—7:30 PM; CLOSED FRIDAY AFTERNOON

You'll pass many shops selling trims along this route. They will all overpower you with their hypnotizing shininess. Oh, those Marrakchi shop owners, they are the original dream merchants. Be aware that 95% of the merchandise is made somewhere far away from this desert city. The 5% genuine, made-in-Morocco trim can be found at Khalid's stall, up the street from Idbelkacem, on the left. The charming man will use Italian as his lingua franca because he spent many years working in Italy.

5. Ben Labhar Adil

45 RUE DU COMMERCE ● NO PHONE
CASH ● 9AM–7:30PM; CLOSED FRIDAY AFTERNOON

ontinue walking up the street until you come to a right turn down a
darkish alleyway. Keep a lookout for this bead shop with entrances
both on the alley and on the street parallel to Hay Salam (which is

the name of the whole area), the Rue du Commerce. Adil's shop is quite large and has the air of a really good craft supply store. It's filled with every color, shape, and size bead made with dyed terra cotta—all are sold by weight. Adil stocks other bead choices and the supplies needed to make your own jewelry.

6. La Cabane d'Ali Baba

53 RUE DU COMMERCE • Tel: 212 061 24 71 35
CASH • 9:00AM–7:30 PM; CLOSED FRIDAY AFTERNOON

Exit Adil through the Rue du Commerce side—you will smell the *rue* before you arrive. There's a wonderful fragrance of mixed spices in the air—one of the benefits of being in an area where cars are restricted. Once on the Rue du Commerce, you should see this stall, overflowing with every imaginable color and shape of bead: silver as large as golf balls; resin ones that resemble amber, turquoise, and ivory; silver amulets and hands of Fatima. Here you can buy assorted beads by the scoopful, whole packets of beads by weight, or strings of beads waiting to be knotted and finished off. While the style is pure North Africa—the beads are all made in China! To be fair—there are some plain, and hennaed horn beads for sale as well—they're local. The owner is very simpatico, so it's hard to resist his wares.

7. Amssilia Hafid

You'll see this smaller bead shop across the *rue* from Ali Baba—you'll recognize it by the rows of black, rough cloth mitts hanging outside the doorway—they are used for scrubbing your body with *savon beldi* while bathing in hammams. Hafid stocks many of the same items as his neighbor, but will sell beads by the piece—rather than by weight. He also has silver-colored fish in various sizes, made with mechour—the non-tarnishing metal. The fish would look just right mixed with a variety of beads made into a necklace for your favorite Pisces.

8. Herboriste El Menkari

20 EL JADIDA ● NO PHONE

9:30AM–7:30PM; CLOSED FRIDAY AFTERNOON

After you leave Hafid, walk to your right down the Rue du Commerce. Take in the sights. There are wonderful spice sellers, and fruit and vegetable stands. Walk until you come to a right turn which will take you back to the busy shopping street—make a quick left then right again. Look for a left turn before you get to the archway—you'll recognize this corner pharmacy by the rows of gold-embossed, midnight-blue apothecary bottles, and the barrels of spices. Just when you think that you can't bear to look at one more natural pharmacy/spice seller, peruse El

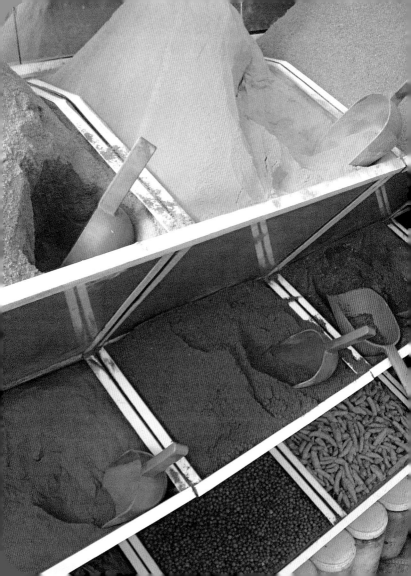

Menkari for a moment. Those beautiful blue bottles contain essential oils. They'll decant as much—or as little—of the oil as you desire. The scents are pure lavender, mint, rose, jasmine, orange flower, and so on. They will grind spices to order. Everything at this stall is very fresh. Check out the powdered, natural pigments—pure color and a great item to purchase. Bring some home and paint your terra cotta flower pots fuchsia and bright yellow.

9. Aya's

11 DERB JDID
Tel: 212 024 38 34 28 ● Cell: 212 061 46 29 16
WWW.AYASMARRAKECH.COM ● MOST CREDIT CARDS
DAILY 9:30AM–12:30PM AND 3–7:30PM

Turn left when you leave El Menkari. Walk under a kind of portico and find Aya's on your left. Aya, the "most beautiful" in Arabic, is named for the beautiful daughter of owner Nawal – who's one of the nicest people that you'll meet in Marrakech (to be sure she's there, call her cell phone first). Nawal grew up in the Mellah carefully observing the button- and trim-makers. Her own clothing line—caftans made with the finest quality linen, cotton, silk, and silk-lined velvet, then exquisitely embellished with subtle, or more intricate trims or embroidery—is not to be ignored. Nawal's keen color sense is evident, for example, in a chocolate-brown linen caftan adorned with robin's-egg blue embroidery. If you find what you like but would prefer it in a different size, or color, or trim—Nawal will happily oblige your wish and then ship it to you. Her thoroughly modern caftans sewn by a women's cooperative in Mauritania are made with filmy tie-dyed cotton. The caftans, which come in various color combinations, are ideal accessories worn over a t-shirt and leggings, or as swimsuit covers. Aya's has some of the nicest caftans, both long and short

for both men and children, in Marrakech. She offers a good supply of small gift items too: vintage Moroccan postcards simply encased in glass, heavily decorated babouches, shawls, and *raiku* pots encircled by snakes.

If you're feeling peckish and in need of refreshment, **Tanjia** ✦ is literally next door to Aya's. Their menu is modern Moroccan and the atmosphere extremely elegant with a very comfortable terrace affording great views of the city—maybe something Edith Wharton might have enjoyed?

10. Abderrazak

DERB JDID ● NO PHONE
9:30AM–7:30PM; CLOSED FRIDAY AFTERNOON

Diagonally across the way from Tanjia is one crazy bead place. Have a quick look—because by now you've probably had it with this stuff. Abderrazak has some pretty inexpensive things including beaded

belts—which look wonderful looped through a pair of jeans—glass beads, painted beads, beaded-rope necklaces, and mirrors. The real treat would be

if you happen to show up in the afternoon when all the women of the family gather to make the products.

11. Artisanat Machmakha

49 PLACE DES FERBLANTIERS ● *Tel:* 212 024 38 92 87
SOME CREDIT CARDS ● DAILY 9:30AM–8PM

o back out under the portico; just after you pass Aya's turn left, then left again into the Place des Ferblantiers. This whole *place* is ringed with metal workers, and shops that sell their wares. Keep to your left when you walk into the square until you come to this shop which should be easy to spot with the copious display of goods in front—including a copper bathtub. Without question Machmakha sells the most refined merchandise in the square. There are lanterns of many designs, torcheres, lamp bases, candlesticks, bottles covered with intricately etched mechour and matching stoppers, garden accessories, sinks, and bathtubs.

Right next door to Machmakha find one of the most acclaimed restaurants in the Mellah, if not all of Marrakech—**Kosybar** ✦, at number 47. Enjoy delicious food and stunning rooftop views—that include the magnificent nesting storks atop the nearby Palais el Badi.

12. Youssef & Abdelhadi

36 PLACE DES FERBLANTIERS ◈ Tel: 212 071 86 47 60
CASH ◈ DAILY 9:30AM–8PM

Leave Machmakha, turn left and walk to the south side of the *place* to find this shop. Youssef sells items made with copper, brass, pewter, and iron: wash basins, mirror frames, and lamps. Actually, lamps are their specialty, especially sconces.

Before you exit the *place*, take a look at the workshop on the north side. This manufacturer of industrial products has piles of Rube Goldberg-esque machines that extract the essence from roses, large containers with conical tops used for displaying spices, and huge storage containers that look like mini-silos. It's a photo op!

Leave the *place* on the left side—the opposite of where you entered. Walk across a somewhat busy intersection and find the entrance to the Marché Couvert on your left. There will be buckets filled with roses and other flowers just under the archway. A trip through this market is one for the curious. The citizens of Marrakech come from all over the city to shop here for fresh fish, fowl, and rabbits. The product displays are startling: heaps of fish still smelling like the Atlantic Ocean, and bunnies munching on clover seemingly without a care in the world. It's yet another photo op.

13. Elmohajiri

139 AVENUE HAUMANN EL FETOUAKI ● **Tel:** 212 024 38 56 58
9:30AM–8PM; CLOSED FRIDAY AFTERNOON

xit the covered market and walk to your left, you'll be on the Avenue Haumann (Hommane on some maps) el Fetouaki. Walk straight until you come to the junction with the Rue Sidi Bou Chouka. On the point of the junction find this well-stocked hardware store. While there will be many along the way, this one seems to be the "go to" store for the owners of some of the most stylish riads in the city. They come for the brass, copper, and wrought-iron door latches, hands of Fatima knockers, covered toilet paper holders, towel racks, curtain rods, wash basins, fireplace accessories, and all the products needed to keep them clean and shiny.

Okay, now it's time to walk back a bit and rejoin Walk 4. Cross to the other side of the avenue and walk to your right until you meet the junction of the Rue Riad Zitoun el Kedim. Turn left onto the *rue*—it's a slightly hidden entrance. You'll know that you're on the correct street when you see shops on both sides selling assorted products made with recycled tires. There are at least five or six shops on this *rue* devoted to the most ingenious picture frames, stools, buckets, jugs, small chests with air valve drawer pulls, flip-flops (just imagine the tread on those!) and of particular interest, bags with perforated designs—all made with recycled tires. Move up and down this short stretch until you find what you like—check out the goods and the prices before you make a deci-

sion. Mixed in amongst the recycled tire shops are ones that sell kitchen equipment and gadgets. As you walk up the street, you'll leave the recycled tire shops and begin to see shops that sell goods made with recycled metal. Even if you don't need a bellows—you might consider one as an objet d'art. Each one is unique. There are window boxes, watering cans, and pails made with sheets of printed metal. As you move along, you'll see a few shops selling Mondrian-ish messenger bags made with pieced-together, primary-colored oilcloth. Continue your stroll until you reach your starting-off point, the Place Jemaa el Fna.

Shops on the Rue Riad Zitoun el Kedim are cash only, and the hours are 9:30am–8pm, daily.

AN ADDITIONAL SMALL WALK

Rue Bab Agnaou

Now, depending on how you're feeling, you can either go home and rest, or take this mini-walk. The enticement for the walk is that the first stop will be one of the best pastry shops/tearooms in the city—a good spot to regroup. If you don't take this little walk now, plan on doing it sometime when you find yourself in the Jemaa el Fna—there are a few great places not to be missed. When you exit the Rue Riad Zitoun el Kedim, turn left and walk around to the very wide Rue Bab Agnaou. This section of the *rue* is completely pedestrian and full of restaurants, snack bars, a large movie theatre, and lots of people. As you walk, stay to the left for the Patisserie des Princes.

14. Patisserie des Princes

32 RUE BAB AGNAOU ● Tel: 212 044 44 30 33
SOME CREDIT CARDS ● DAILY 5AM–10:30PM

This renowned patisserie has an enormous selection of traditional Moroccan cookies and pastries, some French pastries—warm croissants early in the morning—and bread, ice cream, handmade candies, and a charming—and air-conditioned—tearoom in the back. Not to be missed at Les Princes are their mini-*bisteeya*, one of the most sophisticated dishes of the Moroccan kitchen—this flaky pie is filled with chicken, onions, lemony-eggs, and almonds—the top is dusted with cinnamon and sugar.

The combination of savory, sweet, salty, and buttery is sensational—make sure that you're well covered when you eat it! Buy a box of assorted cookies to take home with you. They transport very successfully.

15. Herboristerie Firadous

26 GALERIE ESSALAM. OFF RUE BAB AGNAOU
Tel: 212 024 44 37 44 • SOME CREDIT CARDS
10 AM–9 PM; CLOSED FRIDAY

erboristerie Firadous is on the same side of the street as Les Princes. It's located upstairs in a mini-mall and there's an obvious sign out in front. Once you walk upstairs, Firadous will be on the right. Firadous translates from Arabic as Heaven. After all the pharmacies that you've seen on your walks through souks, know that here, you have arrived in heaven. This is not a glamorous spot, but the products are genuine. The essential oils are startling in their purity. They are thick with fragrance. Firadous's

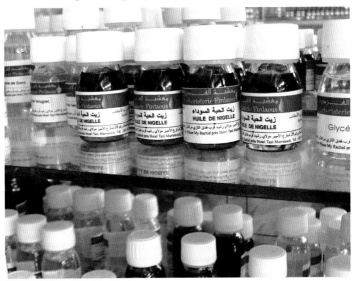

rose water is all you need to keep the skin on your face supple. The obliging "pharmacist," a young and knowledgeable woman, will carefully and patiently answer all your questions. For example, she'll tell how to use the nigella oil to boost your immune system: mix it with honey then drink it with water or milk. She'll measure out as much or as little of the products as you want to purchase.

16. Ryad M

19 RUE DU DISPENSAIRE ● Tel: 212 061 81 56 36
WWW.JNANE.COM ● SOME CREDIT CARDS
DAILY 10:30AM–7:30PM

When you leave the gallery, turn left and continue walking south on the Rue Bab Agnaou for a short distance to the Hotel Tazi. Turn left at the hotel and then almost immediately left on the Rue du Dispensaire. You will find Ryad M at number 19. Ryad M is, coincidentally, the dispensary for Meryanne Loum-Martin's amazing collection of self-designed household goods. French-Senegalese Loum-Martin, a lawyer by training, has become Marrakech's champion of good taste and responsible tourism. Her collections of furniture and lamps incorporate her distinctive motifs—derived from nature—of stars and animal horns. Find the designs perforated into the frames of the furniture or etched into the glass lanterns and lamps and know immediately that it's a Loum-Martin original. There's an outstanding selection of fabrics,

metal and horn bracelets from Senegal, one-of-a-kind hand-dyed silk and velvet shawls, and Meryanne's own line of beauty products called Ethnobotanica. Her husband, Gary Martin, an ethnobotanist, has cultivated all the plants on their out-of-town property from which the stimulating, and at the same time soothing, products are made. Treat yourself to fennel or cinnamon shower gel, or clove shampoo, or ginger massage oil. Ryad M always has a selection of African subject paintings by the Belgian artist Phillipe Deltour. His impressive work is executed on cement bags.

Be sure to check out the website for information about other Loum-Martin projects.

YET ANOTHER SMALL WALK

The Kasbah

The Kasbah—ah, the Kasbah—just saying it immediately conjures a whole panorama of dangerously romantic images. Not this one. It's not even a big shopping area; however, if you find yourself sightseeing at the Tombeaux Saadiens, for example, there are a few spots worth checking out.

1. Complexe d'Artisanat

RUE DE LA KASBAH ● **Tel:** 212 024 38 18 53
CREDIT CARDS ● DAILY 9:30AM–7:30PM

If you're standing in front of the Mosque de la Kasbah or the Tombeaux Saadiens, walk to your right, straight ahead on the Rue de la Kasbah— the enormous Complexe D'Artisanat will be on your right. You may see

several tourist busses parked in front before you actually spot the building. This should in no way be confused with the Ensemble Artisanal. This complex is strictly commercial and crammed full of products. The dizzying selection can be overwhelming—but if you're passing through Marrakech and don't have much time to shop, there's plenty of choice here. The department store-style place is well-staffed and secure for truly hassle-free shopping. Choose from grand assortments of rugs, caftans, modern and antique jewelry, small pieces of furniture with inlaid bone designs, pottery, all sorts of metal objects, leather outerwear – including a service that will make you a leather jacket to size in 24 hours, toiletries including some very pretty wooden kohl containers, poufs, luggage and on and on... souvenirs galore.

2. Temhal M'Bark

BOUTIQUE NUMBER 315, KASBAH ● NO PHONE
CASH ● DAILY 9:30AM–8PM

This gallery/studio of the painter Temhal M'Bark is worth the trip down the Rue de la Kasbah. When you leave the Complexe, turn right and walk down the *rue* a bit. You'll soon recognize the place because it's garlanded with paintings at the opening. There are more stacked on the ground. These very touching primitive paintings that depict everyday aspects of Moroccan life are wonderful souvenirs of your trip. Painted on lightweight wood are simple images of a man getting his hair cut, a woman breast-feeding her baby, children playing, and some of the more recognizable local monuments. The backs of the paintings, covered with verses from the Koran, hold almost as much interest as the front. They are reasonably priced to boot.

Turn around and walk back toward the tombs. Just before you get to the main square, look for a right turn up a little incline. This partially covered street which is lined with butchers, spice merchants, an Internet hotspot, and dry goods stalls will lead you into the fresh produce area of the Kasbah. It's interesting because it's local—there's no playing up to tourists. Of course if you attempt to buy something, you'll more than likely be charged an unrealistic price. Of interest are some of the goods that are laid out on the ground—especially the woman's underwear, some of which look like Pucci pedal pushers.

Open early in the morning until about 9pm—except for the fresh produce sellers who start to pack up mid-afternoon.

WALK № 6

Gueliz

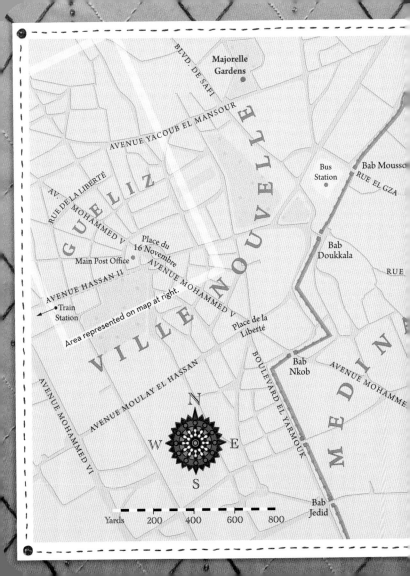

Majorelle Gardens

BLVD. DE SAFI

AVENUE YACOUB EL MANSOUR

Bus Station

Bab Mousso
RUE EL GZA

AV. DE LA LIBERTÉ

RUE DE LA LIBERTÉ

GUELIZ

MOHAMMED V

VILLE NOUVELLE

Place du 16 Novembre

Main Post Office

AVENUE MOHAMMED V

Bab Doukkala

RUE

AVENUE HASSAN II

Train Station

Area represented on map at right.

Place de la Liberté

MEDINA

Bab Nkob

AVENUE MOHAMME

AVENUE MOULAY EL HASSAN

BOULEVARD EL YARMOUK

AVENUE MOHAMMED VI

N
W   E
S

Bab Jedid

Yards   200   400   600   800

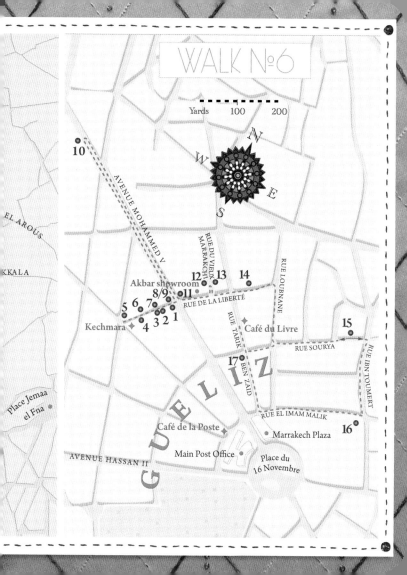

WALK Nº6

Yards   100   200

10

AVENUE MOHAMMED V

EL AROUS

KKALA

RUE DU VIEUX
MARRAKCHI

Akbar showroom

12   13   14

RUE LOUBNANE

8/9   11

5 6 7   RUE DE LA LIBERTÉ

4 3 2 1

Kechmara

RUE TARIK

Café du Livre

15

RUE SOURYA

RUE IBN TOUMERT

G   U   E   L   I   Z

17

BEN ZAID

Place Jemaa
el Fna

RUE EL IMAM MALIK

Café de la Poste

16

Marrakech Plaza

AVENUE HASSAN II

Main Post Office

Place du
16 Novembre

Gueliz is part of la Ville Nouvelle, the new city. Barely 100 years old, this neighborhood situated slightly northwest of the Medina, with its Western-style apartment buildings, and private homes set back off the street surrounded by lush gardens, is an excellent shopping destination away from the chaos of the souks. It's a ten-minute trip by taxi from the Medina. Wherever you're coming from, make sure to get off on the corner of Avenue Mohamed V and Rue de la Liberté in order to begin your adventure. Almost all the shops in Gueliz observe European-style shop schedules; they are open from 9:30am–1pm, then 3:30–7:30pm, and are closed on Sundays. Bargaining is not exactly Gueliz-style. However, if you're buying a quantity of items from a particular shop, you might quietly ask for a discount—if it's not offered first.

1. Place Vendôme

141 AVENUE MOHAMED V ● Tel: 212 024 43 52 63
CREDIT CARDS ● 9:30AM–1PM AND 3:30–7:30PM;
CLOSED SUNDAY

This luxury leather goods store on the corner of Avenue Mohamed V and Rue de la Liberté could be called the Hermès of North Africa. The late Leon Amzallag, and his son Claude, made their shop's reputation as saddle and boot makers. The shop is still stocked with a collection of handsome saddles and they will custom-make a pair of boots for you. All their products are made with soft-as-butter goat- or lambskin leather or suede. The shop's shelves are filled with elegant luggage, wallets, clothing, tote bags, shoulder bags, and handbags—including sweet little drawstring pouches in dreamy pastel colors. Of note, a black leather three-quarter-length toggle coat.

Be sure to check out the early-twentieth-century poster hanging in the front room of the shop—it is Morocco's first advertisement for tourism. Unfortunately, it's not for sale.

2. L'Orientaliste

11 & 15 RUE DE LA LIBERTÉ ● *Tel:* 212 024 43 40 74
CREDIT CARDS ● 9:30AM–1PM AND 3:30–7:30PM;
CLOSED SUNDAY

When you leave Place Vendôme, turn left down the Rue de la Liberté. L'Orientaliste is at number 11 and downstairs at number 15. In true orientalist tradition, this shop carries a grand selection of

antique and vintage furniture, and paintings made or designed by Westerners that pay homage to Eastern cultures. There are marvelous, vintage publicity posters. In an unusual juxtaposition of merchandise, L'Orientaliste also has a reputation for carrying the best artisanal perfume in the city, especially the one made with *fleur d'orange*. They have a nice selection of hand-painted perfume bottles as well.

3. Patisserie Al Jawda

11 RUE DE LA LIBERTÉ ● Tel: 212 024 43 38 97
CASH ● DAILY 8AM–8:30PM

This beautiful little pastry shop shares the same address as L'Orientaliste. Its entrance is apparent by the metal palm tree that stands vigil outside. Madame Hakima Alamy, the dedicated owner of the pastry shop, is a caterer as well. So, you can buy a great variety of Moroccan and French cookies—the *feggas à la crème fraiche* are a specialty, pastries, and cakes. In addition, if you order ahead of time, you can take away a platter of hors d'oeuvre, a selection of Moroccan salads, or an artichoke tagine. If you just want a little souvenir, take away a pound or two of assorted cookies. They're very portable.

4. Mamounia Arts Gallery

7 RUE DE LA LIBERTÉ ● *Tel:* 212 024 42 02 00
CREDIT CARDS ● 9:30AM–1PM AND 3:30–7:30PM;
CLOSED SUNDAY

At number 7, this gallery is set back off the street by a few steps. Once the in-house antiques shop of the famous Hotel Mamounia, the shop moved when the hotel began its extensive renovations (Check out the film *The Man Who Knew Too Much* and hear Doris Day sing "Que Será, Será" at the hotel). They are now very happy in Gueliz and have no

intention of moving back to the hotel. Mamounia Arts Gallery carries antiques of unparalleled beauty. Everything seems to be museum-quality and each purchase is accompanied by a certificate of authenticity. If your heart desires a life-size bronze lion, find one here. There are exemplary, small, beautifully framed Orientalist paintings. There is vintage pottery, arms—in particular daggers in bejeweled sheaths, spectacular Berber jewelry, and a fine collection of Judaica starring a Torah written on gazelle skin. There are silk valances, and double-embroidered silk netting. The prices are not for the faint of heart.

Before you cross the street to continue shopping, stop at **Kechmara** ✦ at number 1 for a quick, energizing shot of espresso. This all-white, 60s-style restaurant/bar with Saarinen chairs, is a great spot to rub shoulders with the glamorous, young Marrakchis.

5. Côte Sud

4 RUE DE LA LIBERTÉ ● **Tel:** 212 024 43 84 48
CREDIT CARDS ● 9:30AM–1PM AND 3:30–7:30PM;
CLOSED SUNDAY

Across the *rue* at number 4 find this shop, one of two owned by the Belgian designer Sabine Bastin. Her products could be called European interpretations of classic Moroccan goods—and some things that <u>should</u> be Moroccan. There are bling-bling-sequined straw bags, and straw bags that have been covered with lacey, crocheted designs. There are

clever teapot-handle holders, and terra cotta body scrubbers covered with brightly colored crocheted cotton. There are appealing babouche carriers identified by the slipper appliqués on the bag.

6. Maison Rouge

6 RUE DE LA LIBERTÉ ✿ *Tel:* 212 024 44 81 30
CREDIT CARDS ✿ 9:30AM–1PM AND 3:30–7:30PM;
CLOSED SUNDAY

Next door, at number 6, is Sabine Bastin's second shop. It's larger than Côte Sud and carries a wider variety of merchandise. Of interest are her tote bags with simple emblems of Moroccan life (babouches,

fezzes, and hands of Fatima) appliquéd on the sides, thick terry cloth robes trimmed with multicolored tiny tassels, pillows of every shape and size—some crowded with appliquéd flowers and some striped, lamps made with tin that looks recycled, and more traditional lamps, tea glasses, and simple glass holders. Lots of little gifty things.

7. Ben Rahal

28 RUE DE LA LIBERTÉ ● *Tel:* 212 024 43 32 73
CREDIT CARDS ● 9:30AM–1PM AND 3:30–7:30PM;
CLOSED SUNDAY

Find this rug merchant in a small shop at number 28. Shopping here may be a tad more expensive than haggling for rugs in the souks (classic though, isn't it?). Every carpet here has already been vetted for its

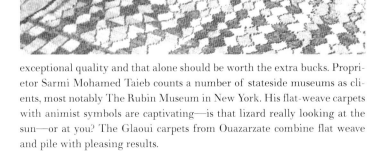

exceptional quality and that alone should be worth the extra bucks. Proprietor Sarmi Mohamed Taieb counts a number of stateside museums as clients, most notably The Rubin Museum in New York. His flat-weave carpets with animist symbols are captivating—is that lizard really looking at the sun—or at you? The Glaoui carpets from Ouazarzate combine flat weave and pile with pleasing results.

139 AVENUE MOHAMED V ● *Tel:* 212 024 43 13 33
CREDIT CARDS ● 9:30AM–1PM AND 3:30–7:30PM;
CLOSED SUNDAY

This shop is on the opposite side of the *rue* from Place Vendôme. There's a very 1950s Fifth Avenue elegance about this shop. You enter and immediately descend a curving staircase to the majority of the merchandise. Downstairs you will find the most elaborate, chicest caftans in the city. Those in the know are aware that if they're coming to Marrakech for a special occasion—say, a wedding—that there's no need to bring an outfit with you. Just make designer Frederique Birkemeyer's Intensité Nomande your first stop after you've gone through customs. The staff will put you at ease and cater to your every wish until you find the caftan of your dreams. In an effort

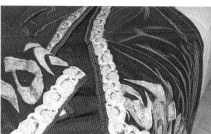

to appeal to the more worldly clients, some of the caftans are styled with narrow shoulders and a more fitted bustline in order for the wearer to maintain a sleek silhouette. There are equally elaborate accessories: belts, handbags, and babouches. They carry a modest but handsome offering of men's cotton shirts. Not everything is as expensive as it sounds—there are some good buys.

9. Kiosque Radouiah

CORNER OF AVENUE MOHAMED V AND RUE DE LA LIBERTÉ
DAILY 8AM–9PM

This newsstand is worth mentioning because it carries the largest selection of foreign newspapers and magazines in the city. They also have guidebooks and maps.

10. Ste Librairie Papeterie Chatr

19–21 AVENUE MOHAMED V ● **Tel:** 212 024 44 79 97
CREDIT CARDS ● 9:30AM–1PM AND 3:30–7:30PM;
CLOSED SUNDAY

Walk north for a few blocks on the avenue to find this very well-stocked book/stationery/art supply store at number 19–21, the only one of its kind in Marrakech. You may wonder if it's worth the few extra blocks just to see another shop that sells maps and guidebooks—well, yes this one is different from the others. The products go be-

yond a very large selection of books on every single Moroccan subject from food to botany. For example, there is a fine collection of Moroccan-subject lithographs and antique prints. As a bonus you'll be passing a number of banks with ATM machines as you walk to the shop—always a necessity when shopping!

11. Atika

34 RUE DE LA LIBERTÉ ● *Tel:* 212 024 43 64 09
CREDIT CARDS ● 9:30AM—1PM AND 3:30—7:30PM;
CLOSED SUNDAY

After you leave the bookshop, cross the avenue and walk south back to the Rue de la Liberté. Turn left into the *rue* and find Atika at number 34. This shoe store sells the most comfortable and beautifully made knockoffs of Prada and Tod's moccasins, and Chanel ballerinas. The leather used for the shoes is sumptuously soft and the color combinations make it nearly impossible to walk out of the store with just one pair. Atika also carries a selection of very simple, classic babouches. There are styles for men, women, and children.

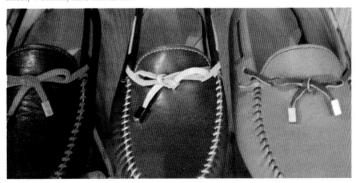

Michèle Baconnier

6 RUE DU VIEUX MARRAKCHI ● Tel: 212 024 44 91 78
WWW.ILOVE-MARRAKESH.COM/BACONNIER
CREDIT CARDS ● 9:30AM–1PM AND 3:30–7:30PM;
CLOSED SUNDAY

urning left when you leave Atika, you'll pass number 42 which is the location of Akbar Delights' showroom—remember them from the Medina? Look for a left turn into a small street, Rue du Vieux Marrakchi. Michèle Baconnier will be on the left at number 6. Madame Baconnier is a Frenchwoman with impeccable taste who's been in business in Gueliz since the 1970s. She is the grande dame of ethnic clothing, accessories, and housewares. Her shop is packed with the latest, most colorful

items: embroidered boots, caftans, kurtas, silk bolero jackets, pastel-colored hobo bags, ballerina babouches in every imaginable color combination, and incredible costume jewelry made with brightly colored stones, gold beads, and braided silk. Her selection of hammam towels—pale yellow with raspberry stripes, white with mint stripes, robin's egg blue with white stripes, and on and on—will leave you wondering how to pack it all.

13. Moor

7 RUE DU VIEUX MARRAKCHI • **Tel:** 212 071 66 13 07
CREDIT CARDS • 9:30AM–1PM AND 3:30–7:30PM;
CLOSED SUNDAY

Just across the way from Michèle Baconnier find Moor, another outpost of the owners of Akbar Delights. Designer Yann Dobry and his sales-director sister, Isabelle Duchet-Annez, define the difference between the merchandise at the two shops when they describe Moor's goods as "urban Moroccan minimalist" as opposed to "busy, colorful souk" like the stuff at Akbar Delights. The caftans, long and short, are made with black, white, or grey raw silk, or rough linen. The decorative embroidery is either the same color as the fabric or black. The round, button-like embroidery that is applied to many of the caftans are called "dollars" in Arabic. There are pillows and bed covers made in the same style as the apparel. Moor is also home to the siblings' collection of images of Mohammed V, the grandfather of the present king of Morocco.

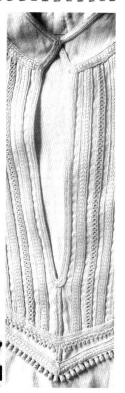

14. Scènes de Lin

Walk back out to the Rue de la Liberté and turn left. Walk down a block or two—Scènes de Lin is hidden behind a thicket of wisteria and bougainvillea vines. Once inside, you are bound to be awed

with the variety of merchandise. Almost everything is made with linen. At Scènes de Lin you can purchase the most exquisite linen bedding with just the right amount of embroidery – and, you can also purchase the bed. There are armchairs and hassocks and pillows covered with simple or elaborate linen, some covered with Fez-style embroidery. There are sorbet-colored linen napkins with embroidered borders. There are really smart, heavily embroidered linen jewelry pouches that make perfect gifts. Downstairs at Scènes de Lin find fabrics sold by the meter. There are solid colors, striped, and embroidered linens and organdie. Scènes de Lin offers a custom curtain-making service. There's a good selection of small things that can be tucked into the corners of your luggage with impunity. Check out the tassels made with raffia.

Alrazal

55 RUE SOURYA ❦ *Tel:* 212 024 43 78 84
CREDIT CARDS ❦ 9:30AM–1PM AND 3:30–7:30PM;
CLOSED SUNDAY

ere's an opportunity to have a look at a bit of the residential area of Gueliz. When you leave Scènes de Lin, turn left, then right at the next cross street, Rue Loubnane. Walk one long block to Rue Sourya, turn left, and walk two blocks to find Alrazal at number 55. Ghizlane Sahli-Sarnefors has designed the most elegantly lyrical collection of children's clothes that you've ever seen — part costume, part really sophisticated gar-

ment. Even if you don't have a child, or a child in your immediate family, you'll find yourself inventing one just so you can buy them a jaunty sailor's blouse, or a mini-caftan, or a corsair's suit with a black jacket heavily embroidered with shades of pink flowers, paired with shocking pink kandrissi—the billowing pants that are gathered to a tight band just below the knee—or an ornate, gold-embroidered dress fit for a princess. Take heart, there are a few items for adults too—that is if you want a raw silk trench coat covered with classic Moroccan embroidery. Who doesn't?

16. Flower Market

CASH ● DAILY, EARLY MORNING TO MID-AFTERNOON

Here's where you have a choice—you can take this longish walk to the very pretty flower market or you can turn around and go to number 17. To get to the market, turn left when you leave Alrazal, then turn right off Rue Sourya into Rue Ibn Toumert. Walk until the Rue Ibn Toumert meets the Rue El Iman Ma-

lik. The flower market, consisting of several stalls, will be on the southwest corner. It's a lively scene. Depending on the day, you may see independent vendors of live peacocks.

17. Mysha & Nito

SOUTHWEST CORNER OF RUE SOURYA AND
RUE TARIK BEN ZAID ● Tel: 212 024 42 16 38
CREDIT CARDS ● 9:30AM–1PM AND 3:30–7:30PM;
CLOSED SUNDAY

Turn left on Rue El Iman Malik and walk a long block to a right turn onto Rue Tarik Ben Zaid. Look for the intersection with Rue Sourya to find the shop. This darkly mysterious store carries signature caftans from Moroccan designers Lhoucine Ait El Medhi and Zahra Yagoubi. They are extremely showy—truly Arabesque—definitely special occasion apparel. Mysha & Nito offers singular jewelry, including a gold outline of a hand of Fatima, housewares, and furniture.

Now, you deserve a quiet, relaxing, tasty meal. **Café du Livre** ✦ is straight ahead at 44 Rue Tarik Ben Ziad. Enter through the courtyard of the Patio Hotel Toulousain and go upstairs. The Café has WiFi, a lending library, and the latest magazines and newspapers as well as a very comfortable restaurant. Their signature salad with cabbage, goat cheese, caramelized onion, raisins, almonds, and croutons hits the spot. But if it's a burger and fries that you crave, they can accommodate you. Finish your meal with local yogurt topped with Moroccan honey served in a terra cotta pot, or a slice of lemon tart with nougat ice cream. Café du Livre is open from 8am to midnight every day. (Tel. 212 024 43 21 49, credit cards accepted.)

When you leave the café, turn right on the *rue*—you'll meet Rue de la Liberté very quickly. Turn left and walk to Avenue Mohamed V to flag down a taxi to take you home.

Other Places to Check Out in Gueliz

Across Avenue Mohamed V from the Central Post Office, find the city's first shopping mall—Marrakech Plaza. You'll immediately recognize the familiar arches of McDonald's and a large Zara clothing and housewares store. Of interest in the Plaza is **Patisserie 16** ✦ with its grand selection of delicious French pastries.

Across from the Post Office on its northern side find the **Café de la Poste** ✦. With its wide veranda and ceiling fans, you just might expect to see Humphrey Bogart in one of his most famous roles, Rick from *Casablanca*, leaning against the bar. The menu is the usual selection of Moroccan and international dishes. Atmosphere is topnotch.

WALK №7

Sidi Ghanem or
La Zone Industrielle

Find this Moroccan version of an industrial park populated with warehouses, showrooms, and workshops of some of the finest contemporary designers in the city about eight miles northwest of town. The area is trolled by the foremost interior decorators in Marrakech. Take a taxi out there and ask to be brought into the *zone* through the second entrance (there are three), turn left, and get off at number 277, Amira, on the right side. Wherever you start your stroll, be sure to pick up a map of the area—they're available everywhere. When your walk is finished, ask someone in the last shop that you've visited to call a car for you. Of course, you could hire a car and driver for the day and make the rounds of some of the other destination spots as well.

There's lots to see. Here are a few of the more notable places.

Take note that the retail hours that are observed by the majority of the showrooms are 9:30am–1pm, 2:30–6pm, Monday through Friday. Some places are open on Saturday. Just about everyone will ship your purchases.

1.

Amira

#277 SIDI GHANEM ❧ Tel: 212 024 33 62 47
WWW.AMIRABOUGIES.COM ❧ CREDIT CARDS

Enter this ultra-modern showroom with dark eggplant-colored floors and walls and find yourself in a wonderland of candles. Gigantic candles that resemble the pillars of Stonehenge, candles as vases with smaller candles inside, small flower-shaped candles that float in a wax basin, and candles in tea glasses with tasseled trims all in the must-have colors of orange, purple, fuchsia, and lime green. There are bases for candles and books about candles.

Next door to Amira is the lovely, little **Café Cosaque** ✦. The café opens at 8am and closes at 4pm. Stop by for refreshments as you peruse the zone.

2. Chez Zoe

#510 SIDI GHANEM • **Tel: 212 061 37 20 99** • CREDIT CARDS

- -

Diagonally across the street from the café find a cul-de-sac and #510, Chez Zoe. Chez Zoe is the showroom and work space where every single product sold by the Hamille sisters is made. Caroline, a former dancer in France, oversees the manufacture of the made-to-order bedding for hotels around the world, and for private clients. The top-quality, hand-stitched sheets and pillowcases come with a variety of embroidered borders. The super-thick terry cloth djellabahs/bathrobes and superb bath towels come in soft colors like white, sand, and ivory and all are trimmed with classic Moroccan embroidery.

You will have the opportunity to observe the ladies who patiently sew the goods.

3. L'Atelier

#294 SIDI GHANEM ● **Tel: 212 024 35 62 06**
EMAIL: LATELIERHOME@YAHOO.FR ● **CREDIT CARDS**

Leave Chez Zoe, walk back to the main drag and turn left. It will be a short walk to L'Atelier. This is the showroom/workshop of long-time Marrakech resident and French designer Corinne Bensimon. Her claims-to-fame are beautiful window treatments made to your specs with linen or cotton fabric in one of the subtle colors from her strictly-observed palette. The curtains, like so many of her other home furnishings, are embellished with simple embroidery or silkscreen images from vintage photographs of Moroccans. Bensimon carries her own line of lamps as well: standing, chandeliers, and table. There are some easy-to-carry-home pillows, and teapots for sale too.

4. Peau d'Ane

#297 SIDI GHANEM ● **Tel: 212 024 33 65 50**
WWW.PEAUDANE.DE ● CREDIT CARDS

Next door to L'Atelier find this showroom that carries monumentally-sized home furnishings. If you're decorating a palace – or a huge loft, you'll be happy with the sculptural floor lamps, hammered metal disks as large as small planets, sub-Saharan wood carvings, hammered metal poufs with leather tops, stools, and what appear to be umbrella stands, but—because it rarely rains in Marrakech—call it a walking stick stand, or a base for a cocktail table.

5. Lilo

#310 SIDI GHANEM ● **Tel: 212 074 02 04 25** ● CREDIT CARDS

Down the street from Peau d'Ane, set back a bit at #310, find the showroom of the very hip clothing line, Lilo. They call themselves, "glamour wear and colorful design." Define Lilo's "colorful" as interesting design, not necessarily composed of varied colors. This collection of black, white, and khaki safari jackets with images of skulls and roses silk-screened on the sleeves and back, metallic-leather babouches, ceramic jewelry, and soft black, gold-embellished tote bags, among other stylish merchandise, could be called Marrakech hip-hop.

6. Akkal

#322 SIDI GHANEM ❧ Tel: 212 024 33 59 38
WWW.AKKAL.NET ❧ CREDIT CARDS

A few hundred yards away find this ceramics showroom, the pioneering business of the industrial zone. Akkal, which translates from the Berber dialect as "earth," makes all of their pottery in Marrakech. The sleek shapes and incredibly rich colors—all found in nature—combine to make some sort of purchase at Akkal inevitable. Among the choices:

tagine and other covered dishes, dinner plates, soap dishes, teapots, coffee-pots, salad bowls, ceramic tea glasses (irresistible), slender flat-sided vases which look terrific in groups of seven or nine, pitchers with metallic glazes, and incense holders. Surely, there's something for you.

7. Nihal

#366 SIDI GHANEM ● Tel: 212 071 16 01 62 ● CREDIT CARDS

It might be worth your while to call for a car at Akkal and have them drive you to this weaver's atelier. It's a bit of a hike from the other places. The driver shouldn't have a problem waiting while you visit Nihal. Marion Verdier, the owner/designer of this *atelier de tissage* Marrakech" has created a terrific collection of wall hangings, curtains, pillows, lamp shades, tote bags, simple furniture covered in her fabric, and fabric by the meter.

You'll find fabrics that are knotted, laser-cut cotton, thin wool basket weaves, tufted cotton, sheer silk netting, and leather weaves all loomed, colored, and sized to order.

Ask to see the weavers' room. Fascinating.

OTHER DESTINATIONS

Jardins Majorelle

AVENUE YACOUB MANSOUR ● Tel: 212 044 30 18 52
WWW.JARDINMAJORELLE.COM ● CREDIT CARDS
DAILY: SUMMER 8AM–6PM, WINTER 8AM–5PM

Perhaps the most gloriously original spot in Marrakech, the Majorelle gardens offer the visitor a view into the deliriously colorful world of the early-twentieth-century painter Jacques Majorelle. You will marvel at the plots of cacti and succulents, bowers of bougainvillea, and at the startlingly rich colors—lemon yellow, cerulean blue, fuchsia, truly orange orange, and the purple-tinged cobalt blue known as *bleu Majorelle*—applied to the planters, pathways, and buildings on the property. One of the gardens' buildings houses a jewel-box-like boutique filled with beautiful Moroccan arts and crafts made by artisans who work exclusively for the shop. The design is overseen by the shop's creative director, Bernard Sanz, a veteran of the French fashion business who worked with St. Laurent (whose foundation oversaw the restoration of the gardens and continues to maintain them), as well as Balmain and Hermès. His meticulous attention to detail and desire to maintain the integrity of the gardens in the selection of

merchandise offered for sale gives the consumer choices unlike any other—anywhere—not just Marrakech. There are caftans and babouches made with the famously flowered fabric from Liberty of London. There are very stylish bags made with recycled plastic by 22 women living in an ecologically-sound village outside of Marrakech. There is pottery, made by women from the northern part of the country, using a method and designs that date back to the Peloponnesian era. There are tablecloths from Fez with double-faced embroidery—each side takes four months to stitch. Sanz says that "owning a piece like this is to own an exceptional artisanal piece—even the fabric is handwoven." There is a singular wedding dress embroidered with Arabic love poems at its edges. There is a tiny art gallery within the shop

that has a beautiful collection of vintage and antique prints featuring garden subjects. Also included is a collection of sepia-toned photographs of North Africa. There are candles, books, and small leather accessories.

For the intrepid, the gardens are a short hike from the northern part of Gueliz. Otherwise take a cab. There is a beautiful outdoor café within the gardens, so plan to visit around breakfast time for a delightful *petit déjeuner* of freshly squeezed orange juice, mint tea, and Moroccan crepes—or, at lunchtime for a fresh salad, sandwich, or tagine—or at teatime for the Coupe Majorelle, a concoction of date, orange blossom, and vanilla ice cream topped with copious amounts of whipped cream and dates—all before, or after, your tour of the gardens and shopping adventure.

Bab El Khemis Flea Market, The Thursday Market

BAB EL KHEMIS IS LOCATED AT THE NORTHEAST CORNER OF
THE CITY, A RIGHT TURN OFF THE ROUTE DE FEZ.
CASH • DAILY 9:30AM–6PM

Wake up early in the morning, have breakfast—get yourself to the flea market, just outside the walls of the Medina, no later than 9:30am. Find the goods at this Thursday and Sunday market laid out on a sidewalk along the ramparts, just slightly south of the gate Bab el Khemis. Treasures abound but you will need to sift through mountains of junk, and have the fortitude to elbow your way past competing scavengers, ahem, dealers. If you have a well-trained eye, you will be able to spot prayer beads from the south of the country, vintage Berber rugs, old pottery from Fez and Safi, vintage caftans, and architectural salvage buried beneath old TV antennas, rusty bicycles, cheap rugs from China, and plastic flowers. It's a lot of work. But, oh, what satisfaction when you discover that jewel.

Back up to the gate, Bab el Khemis. Go through it and there you will find a permanent flea market—actually a souk with stalls. Find sellers of old teapots, rugs, furniture, bric-a-brac (a vintage alarm clock stopped at 10:30), architectural salvage, and stacks and stacks of unglazed pottery. The souk is interesting, but the Thursday and Sunday markets are down-right exciting. It's the thrill of the hunt!

Village du Poterie

Get back into your car or a cab and head south from the flea market to this strip of ten pottery workshops/showrooms on the Boulevard du Golf Souk at a crossroads marked by a huge Station Africa gas station. The selection is enormous, so you might want to focus on two or three places: Poterie d'Or, Poterie du Golf, and Chez Abdou. They all carry tagine dishes but Poterie d'Or's are the plain, classic glazed terra cotta. Poterie du Golf specializes in glazed and decorated products. Find decorated tagine dishes, plates, and bowls in all shapes and sizes, some adorned with traditional patterns from Safi. Find olive oil bottles, tiny tagine dishes to use as salt cellars, and candlesticks. Find dishes decorated with olives that <u>are</u> for holding olives with a section to deposit the pits. At Chez Abdou find urns and pots covered with the mosaic-like tile work called zellij. There are pots and urns that are finished with the process called tadlekt in which the surface is covered with a coating of powdered limestone to which color pigment is added. The surface is sealed with eggwhites, then polished with an oil-based soap—like *savon beldi*—until a dull sheen is achieved. The finished product is impermeable to moisture.

Make sure to walk to the back of the showrooms to have a look at the workshops.

All of the shops ship. You could furnish an entire patio or terrace, or add accents to your in-ground garden with a selection of pots from these artisans.

Promark

GALERIE HERITAGE, ROUTE DE CASABLANCA
Tel: 212 024 44 98 ● SOME CREDIT CARDS
DAILY 9AM–12:30PM AND 2:30–7PM

ind this wholesaler of household goods near the supermarket, Marjane. If you're moving to Marrakech, opening a guesthouse, or restaurant, then this is the place for all your furnishings. Or, if aisles and aisles of goods at reasonable prices interest you – then go. Aside from appliances, there are plates and bowls of every description, notably traditional

blue and white Moroccan patterns, and plain white. There are mechour (the non-tarnishing metal that looks like silver) tagine dishes, trays, and teapots. There are fancy tea glasses, and that wonderful flatware with the glass-beaded handles that you saw at Berrada (page 56). No surprise, the Berrada family owns Promark.

Marjane

ROUTE DE CASABLANCA
YOU CAN TAKE BUS #13 FROM THE MAIN POST OFFICE IN
GUELIZ; MARJANE IS THE LAST STOP. ● Tel: 212 044 31 37 24
CREDIT CARDS ● DAILY 9AM–8PM

ind this *hypermarché* further north on the Route de Casablanca. The Marjane supermarkets are the largest chain in Morocco. This particular market is in a shopping mall that includes a McDonald's, United Colors of Benetton, and Pepe Jeans among other shops that you should be able to live without while in Marrakech. However, Marjane is interesting. In some of the aisles of this clean, well-organized store, find made-in-Morocco products that make perfect gifts: honey, jams, tea, wine, the all-important argan oil, toiletries, and the accessories that you need to make perfect mint tea. For immediate consumption, make sure to look in the dairy aisle for exceptional yogurt and local cheese.

ACKNOWLEDGMENTS

• • • • •

I f serendipity can be considered a force, it was precisely the action of chance that drove this guide. I had casually mentioned to Angela Hederman, the Little Bookroom's publisher, that Marrakech is a great shopping city and before I knew what was happening I was on a plane heading toward the great trading post-oasis of Morocco. Angela has been a superb custodian of this project. Tamar Elster, Tim Harris, Linda Hollick, and Jacquelyn Moorad at the Little Bookroom have assisted with care. Adrian Kitzinger made easy-to-follow maps for the fortunate traveler.

You'd think that Louise Fili and Jessica Hische were at my side throughout my meanderings through the souks of Marrakech by the distinct and precisely Marrakchi design they created for this guide.

Old friend Nally Bellati not only took all the photographs, but cheered me on every day as we set out to discover the treasures of the city. Elena Masera and Maryam Montague were tireless and kind guides to their adopted home.

Without hesitation, John Derian opened the doors of his Kasbah riad giving us a real oasis within the oasis. Super, "super", José Lévy made sure that once we arrived at the oasis everything worked like a charm.

While just about everyone that I encountered in Marrakech was generous with their time and information there were a few who gave above and beyond; Yann Dobry, Meryanne Loum-Martin, Madison Cox, Bernard Sanz, Michèle Baconnier, Corinne Bensimon, Mustapha Blaoui, and Nawal El Hriti.

Before I embarked on this shopping adventure, in New York, Del Blaoui spent hours with me outlining places of interest in his native city.

To everyone, Shukran, Merci Beaucoup, Thank You Very Much.

INDEX

ABOUT the AUTHOR

• • ● • •

Susan Simon is the author of five cookbooks including *The Nantucket Table* and *The Nantucket Holiday Table*. She writes a bi-monthly food chat column for *The Nantucket Inquirer & Mirror* and contributes to *Nantucket Today*. She is a caterer and event planner in New York City.

Visit her website at
WWW.SUSANSIMONSAYS.COM

ABOUT the PHOTOGRAPHER

• • ● • •

Italian photojournalist Nally Bellati has contributed photographs and features to major Italian magazines. She works as a photographer for fashion houses and design companies. Her book *New Italian Design* has been translated into four languages.

Her blog can be found at
HTTP://CONTESSANALLY.BLOGSPOT.COM